Roam Free:
A Travel Transformation Memoir

By Charlotte Tweed

Roam Free: A Travel Transformation Memoir

Published by Follow It Thru Publishing

www.heatherandrews.press
www.followitthrupublishing.com
http://www.getyouvisible.com/

Print ISBN: 9781513655680
eBook ISBN: 9781513655673

Head shot photography by Jenna Brownlee

Dedication

Every day I write out my gratitudes and thank God for all He has blessed me with: Darryl, my loving and adoring husband; Brandon, our son and light of my life; Daren, my supportive big brother; Rita and Ken, caring in-laws; Blaine, who treated me like a daughter, we miss you; and for Dad. Time spent with you in your golden years has been far different than childhood. Because of you and Mom, I am who I am today.

Certain names have been changed to respect confidentiality.

Table of Contents

Foreword

I have spent about a decade travelling and living in other countries and it has completely changed my life. What I learned in those ten years about myself and the world changed me forever. Through travelling abroad, I gained a deeper appreciation of people who are different from me, the beauty of cultural diversity, and was constantly challenged to think about my ideas, spirituality, and long held beliefs about the world in general. To say that experiencing the world has affected me may be a bit of an understatement.

I have met countless people I respect and admire since arriving back in North America. Charlotte Tweed is one of those people. Every time I've met with Charlotte there's an extraordinary look in her eyes. The kind of look that has me believing she's up to something big and beautiful. As long as I've known her, she has been compelled to pursue something far more vast and wild than many others are willing to accept in life. Charlotte has proven she has the tenacity needed to achieve her goals and to expand her own horizons.

A few years ago, when I suggested that Charlotte and Darryl should take off for six months of travel to discover what it might do for their business, I had no idea what that singular suggestion would turn into. What I did know was two things: 1) Charlotte would be willing to tackle the challenges of long-term travel even though other people might see it as crazy; and 2) The experience would change her and her husband forever. It delights me every time I imagine all the potential risks Charlotte was willing to tackle in order to chase her goals.

New experiences change us, Charlotte writes, because they force us out of what we know and help us ask questions of life and of ourselves. I wish I had read a book like *Roam Free* earlier in my life. I might have been willing to leave my fears and embrace my curiosity years ahead of when I finally did. This book teaches us to engage more fully in the cultures we journey through. *Roam Free: A Travel Transformation Memoir* might just inspire you to focus on what you truly want in life rather than simply following the mainstream path.

I encourage you, as you read this book and explore Charlotte's stories of travel, be willing to 'risk' what is a 'normal' life for something far more than you can possibly imagine. If this book inspires your latent travel dreams, I urge you to book your next ticket. No one has ever bragged, after all, about how safe and unexciting their life has been. You will not regret the experiences you are about to have. So go forth – roam free!

- Mark Frentz, Executive Coach, Mark Frentz Coaching

Chapter 1

No Turning Back

We entered our very own twilight zone at 1:00 am, Central Africa time zone. The feeling was surreal that we were in Cairo, Egypt; a country I had dreamed of seeing all my life. And now here I was with my husband Darryl, finally and truly here on Egyptian turf. The airport felt like so many other airports at first— bland colours, booming voices over fuzzy speakers, and throngs of people and baggage everywhere. Unbeknownst to us, that was the last feeling of familiarity we would have for many months.

At the forefront of our minds was purchasing our tourist visa. The line was short with only one person in front of us. *So far, so good.* What awaited us later at the luggage carousel would be a very different story. We knew we had to purchase a tourist visa upon arrival, for without one, a tourist is not allowed into the country of Egypt. A visa can be purchased ahead of time but a friend had visited Egypt the year before and said the process was as easy as pie. The visa is US$25 per person, payable in cash only. When we reached the visa counter, I handed the customs agent five ten-dollar American bills, when he abruptly pushed two of them back at me over the counter. The customs agent had dark, slicked back hair and a moustache; his belly bulged slightly, straining the buttons on his white uniform. No smile was on his face or reflected in his eyes. He was deadly serious and was there to perform a job, nothing more. "What's wrong with these?" I asked as I slid the bills back over the counter toward him again.

"Too old. No good." Impatience drew lines on his forehead and around his mouth as he pursed his lips together, squinting at me under his furrowing brow. *Too old? No good? What in the world is he talking about*, I thought as panic fluttered in my stomach. Reasoning with him seemed futile. We had withdrawn US$300 for emergency purposes from our bank in Calgary before leaving. Carrying a small amount of cash is a necessity when travelling in case bank machines don't work in other countries. As we had learned from our pre-trip research, some places only accept cash and if you don't have any bills, you could find yourself stranded. *Why would our bank give us old, useless bills?* Good thing I had more bills of varying ages so I gave him two newer editions. He took those and put our visas in our passports. A flood of excitement and relief rolled over me like a tidal wave. *We made it to Egypt.*

Note to Self: Ensure the bills you bring
next time are brand spanking new.

On to get our luggage. There were no formed lines leading to the luggage pickup area. People were clumped together like a herd of cattle headed toward a branding chute. Like docile cows ourselves, we let the crowd carry us toward our luggage, which was, blessedly, waiting for us at the end of the line. Darryl and I, with luggage in hand, passed through the second stage of customs with no incident and stepped outside. Twilight Zone part two.

It was June in Cairo—dark, dry, and hot. Ramadan had just ended and there were crowds of people outside the airport mingling on the street. Ramadan is a time of quiet, fasting and reflection for Muslims everywhere, while post-Ramadan is a time of celebration and socializing. A blue metal chain link fence separated us from the rest of Egypt. The fence was in place to keep the people arriving by air separated from the throngs of people waiting for their loved ones. It provided some sort of order for people exiting the airport. If the fence was not in place, I imagine nobody would be able to physically leave the Cairo airport for the wall of bodies outside. We were on the inside of the fence next to the airport doors. People clung to the outside of the fence, anxiously looking over one another's shoulders to see if their guests had arrived. The only words we could make out from the crowd came from people on our side of Egypt— inside the fence— calling to us, "Taxi! Taxi!" Our tour operator had warned us not to take any cabs at the airport and to walk right by them when they were trying to solicit us for a ride. We had booked our time in Egypt with a local tour operator so we had our own private driver and private tour guide for our ten-day stay. *Our driver was supposed to meet us outside the airport but how in the world will we find him in this sea of people?* My eyes scanned the crowd. A lump formed in my throat as bits of paranoia found their way into my mind. Then the "what ifs" started. *What if he doesn't show up? What if we are stuck in the airport overnight? What if we can't get to our hotel?* Overwhelming anxiety started to pour into me from my head down to my toes. I was afraid.

There we stood; two pale-faced, blonde Canadians with our deer-in-the-headlights looks. Clutching our suitcases, our eyes searched for our driver amongst the multitude of people that we sensed might devour us if we got closer. *What in the world had we just gotten ourselves into? How did we ever think we could be professional long-term world travellers for six whole months?* Canada, the comforts of home and family, seemed so far away. Even the cold weather we had left back home seemed warm and inviting in comparison to the arid heat bearing down on us more each minute.

Welcome to Egypt. There is no turning back now.

Part 1 – Caterpillar

Chapter 2

Sucker Punch

"HAVE YOU TALKED TO YOUR BROTHER?" was the text message glaring back at me as I checked my cell phone at work that dreadful day. Something was wrong. Darryl had never sent me a text message in all caps before. This was urgent and I knew he needed to talk to me right away. I had been covering for a coworker who was on vacation, so I was not at my desk. Darryl was desperately trying to get ahold of me.

"No," I messaged back, too afraid to add, "why?"

"Your mom had a stroke," was his blunt reply. Leave it to my Darryl to always tell it straight and clear. I put my phone down, turned around in my chair to face my coworkers and repeated the phrase out loud to them, as if I couldn't believe it unless I said it out loud.

"My mom had a stroke." Gasps filled the cubicles around me. Yvonne, a coworker and friend, rushed over to me. "Oh. You poor thing," she said as she wrapped her arms around me in a tight hug. *I have to get out of here*, was all I could think. *I have to get to my mom before she dies. Except how am I going to do that when she lives over 800 kilometres away from me? Why do we have to live in a country that is so vast that we all live so far apart?*

The severity of what had happened started to settle in moment by moment. I thrust some files in my desk drawer, quickly put on my jacket and grabbed my purse. There was no time to pass off duties to anyone else. Time was of the essence. Iris, another coworker and friend, drove me to my husband's work so we could get packed and go to Saskatchewan—eight exasperating hours of driving away.

It was December 22, 2011, and my life would never be the same. They always say it takes an extreme event to bring about change and "they" are right. "They" are always right. The day Mom had a stroke was the day my life was thrown into turmoil. As I look back, it seemed nothing went right for years after this event. I was about to be put through a crucible that would change the way I looked at life and how I lived it.

Mom's health was rated critical by the doctors and for a few days she walked a fine line between this world and the next. She was in and out of consciousness. Her speech was reduced to two words, "yes" and "no," but even they were messed up. No meant yes and yes meant no. Her breathing became laboured as fluid started to set in her lungs. She would cough and choke up mucous. The medical personnel were concerned that pneumonia might settle in. We didn't know if she would make it.

After close to four months in the hospital and a month in rehabilitation, she made a miraculous recovery. I was not present for much of Mom's recovery since I lived so far away. When I saw her at Easter, I could not believe my eyes when she stood up and walked to the door to greet me. She pushed herself back from the kitchen table and stood up with confidence. Her white, floor-length flannel nightgown made her look like an angel. As I put down my bag a smile erupted on my face. The shock of seeing her up and looking well brought tears of joy to my eyes. You wouldn't even know she had suffered a stroke. Mom smiled back at me with the most beautiful smile; a smile that radiated the miracle she had become. Her walk with death was long gone. Slowly, she shuffled over to give me a welcome hug, her bare feet almost gliding on the laminate floor. Wrapping my arms around her without leaning over a hospital bed or a wheelchair was a sensation I thought I might not experience again.

"I knew Charlotte would cry when she saw me get up and walk," Mom said, as my eyes filled with happy tears. A Mother's intuition is always right.

On the night of her stroke, I had prayed that God would grant me one more conversation with Mom. More time was all I wanted. Visiting at the kitchen table and making Mom laugh were my favourite things to do with her. She loved listening to stories from her kids. Experiencing her warm embrace when we would arrive home for a visit always made me feel good inside. Reading over recipes together and deciding what to make for meals while we were home were all things I hoped to cherish again. The small, intimate moments of quality time that are so special between a mother and her child. Those were the moments I longed for. God granted me time and much more. I had my mom back. Well, mostly back—she was never quite the same after her stroke. There were changes in her mannerisms and a slight difference in her speech. But what mattered most was that she was alive and well.

Mom loved to cook. Before the stroke she made delicious, salt-of-the-earth, made-with-love meals. My favourite was roast pork, carrots, and mashed potatoes. Whenever we came home to visit, she always asked what we were hungry for. Baking was a hobby of hers as well. I think she did this more for herself as my family didn't have a sweet tooth. After the stroke, she never cooked her big meals again. I missed Mom's home cooking. In an attempt to make up for this loss, I helped cook the meals when we were at their house.

On my first visit back home, I was determined to teach Mom how to make healthy meals for her and Dad. Armed with my resilience to combat Mom's stubbornness, I began my health food talk.

"Mom, you need to use less salt, butter, and cream when you cook." She stopped me right there.

"I know how to cook healthy. I don't want to cook healthy. All I could think about when I was in the hospital was eating butter and cream again." *Mom's stubbornness: score 1. My attempt at health food: score 0. Okay, so much for that pep talk.*

Talking to Mom on the phone was also a challenge. She would struggle to get the words out sometimes and I think this was because she could not see my face. When we were together and she could see me, see my lips move, see my expressions, she had no issues. Mom wasn't a big talker. She loved to listen and laugh when we would sit around the table and visit. She still loved to spend time with us and listen to what was going on in our lives but she was now a little quieter—almost shy and slightly childlike in her actions. I didn't let this bother me. Mom was different. She'd been through a massive ordeal and was still here. For that, I was grateful.

We continued to go home as often as we could when work allowed. It was a delicate balancing act to work full-time, and use a large portion of our time off to see family. Mom and Dad were now in an apartment rather than a house, so sleeping arrangements were a little less convenient and comfort was a little more elusive. Space was limited when an extra three people came to stay. When unwelcome changes happen we have to learn to roll with the punches. Another uppercut was about to pummel our lives from an unlikely source.

******

I had been working for the health region in Red Deer, Alberta for eight years. Government is famous for constant restructuring. A new Premier had come into power so everyone knew there would be changes in health care—there always is. A wise man I once worked with said, "If anyone mentions restructuring again, I'll run away with my hair on fire." The former health regions were going to be merged into one massive health region for the entire province of Alberta. The region I worked for had a mere ten thousand employees. This was now going to change to ninety thousand employees province-wide. *How could this possibly work?* I don't think anyone had the answer but the restructuring happened anyway.

I was a Human Resources Technician, a position unique in all the province. I loved my job. I had always wanted to work in HR. My workload was perfect and I had every Friday off. It was my privilege to provide excellent customer service to my portfolio of managers. I was a problem solver and if I could help you and make your life easier, my day was good. Collaboration with my coworkers was fulfilling and fun. Carl, my partner in crime—in the life of an HR Tech—was an absolute scream to work with. He would tell me stories of his life back home in a little hick town in Alberta. Countless times, he would have me laughing so hard that I couldn't talk—the tears rolling down my face in rivers.

Jan, Carl and I would go and eat lunch in the park near our office in the warm summer days. Jan was my dear friend that worked in the HR file room. She had a kind heart and inquisitive soul—just my kind of person. Summer is so short in Central Alberta that we simply had to take advantage of it. Off we would go with a gold lamé tablecloth to cover the grungy tables, some other kind of cheap green cloth to cover the dirty benches, and a small dust broom to sweep the leaves and bird poop off the tabletop before draping our chic ornamental cover over top. We didn't mind that homeless people often hung out in the park. We saw one guy move into the forest one day. He tossed a couple of garbage bags over the fence, all the while complaining that his dad threw him out because he was a useless lowlife. Add some colourful language in too, if you please. Oh, and there was a needle-drop nearby. It all added to the charm of the place. Life was good—until restructuring happened.

My HR Tech team was a combination of payroll and labour relations. The team I worked with before the restructuring was an excellent group of people with an incredible knowledge base on the collective agreements for our region. We got along well and enjoyed our workdays together.

Since our team was unique, we didn't fit into the future structure. The writing was on the wall when upper management moved us to another building, away from the hospital. We knew we would be eliminated; we just didn't know when. Then the dreaded day came. We were told our whole department and all of payroll were going to be laid off. Two years working notice was given to us with the chance to apply, and supposedly be the first people chosen for, other positions within HR. All would be fine— or so we thought. The next day, HR instituted a hiring freeze. *Not good.*

Positions dried up. Posted jobs were generally temporary. New positions were slowly being created to fill in the gaps left by our displacement. The problem? There were not enough jobs for all the displaced people. Our team eagerly awaited the postings, certain we would get roles similar to the ones we had. The people in charge had other ideas. I received my phone call on a Friday. "Hello, Charlotte. You have not been chosen for one of the positions, so now we can part ways and you can start down another road." The voice on the other end was cold and callous. It sounded evil without empathy to my ears. I could not believe what was being said to me. *I didn't get a job? How could this be? I was an excellent employee. Wasn't I?* Customer service was of utmost importance to me. I knew my job well, got along with others, and rarely called in sick. *How could this be happening?* My jaw dropped. My eyes widened. My hand clenched the phone in disbelief, squeezing it harder than my heart was beating. My stomach plummeted and I felt sick. The breath left my lungs and speech eluded me. I had just received a sucker punch right to the gut. Fear gripped my mind. *What am I going to do now?* With that one phone call from a manager, my identity had been ripped away from me.

Only a handful of the HR Technicians got jobs after restructuring. The work environment quickly became toxic. The exiles who didn't get spots had to work alongside those that did. Our replacements would call us to ask us how to do the work we used to do. Finally, we just quit answering our phones. We had been promised "meaningful work" over the next two years while we tried to find new arrangements. Meaningful for me meant sitting at my desk and making paperclip necklaces. Others chose to do crossword puzzles. There was nothing for us to do. Absolutely nothing. So, we tried to pass the days in any way possible while still maintaining our sanity.

A group of us got together and decided to create the "Misfits Club." Back in the good old days, we used to have birthday parties and potluck lunches. These get-togethers were a thing of the past and we missed them. There was a new HR Party Planning Committee but we wanted no part of hobnobbing with those undesirables. So, those of us that were displaced started our own party group. I guess you could say it was a closed gang without the tattoos. To feel appreciated and human again, we would celebrate our birthdays and have potlucks on holidays. We became kindred spirits. Stuck together in the cesspool, we built our own raft. A raft that would protect us from the sewers surrounding our desks.

Finally, the two-year stretch of our working notice was up. The banished were praying for a severance package. I was the first one to meet with HR on the day that could manifest pure bliss or utter disappointment. My mouth was dry and my tongue stuck to the roof like hot, melted wax. I was sweating profusely. I walked into the office and sat down with two representatives from HR.

"May I say if this situation ever happens again, do not give a two-year working notice period. It made life hell." I stated plainly to HR Rep #1.

"I agree," she said. "It only made the situation more difficult for everyone and caused the whole department to fester." She slid a brown manila envelope across the table and set it in front of me. With shaking hands, I opened the package.

"We are offering full severance," she stated. My heart began to beat faster. I flipped through the pages as I only cared about the dollar amount. Nothing else mattered to me. Severance would provide me with a cushion to start my own business. Starting a business is a grueling affair, straining not just on finances but on time as well. Having a severance package nest egg would, I hoped, help cover expenses to get our real estate business up and running. It would provide the time I needed to work from home and get our first deal done.

"This is what I was hoping for." I took my papers, put them back in the envelope and walked out of the office. *Hallelujah. My prayers had been answered. Freedom.* Now, everything would be alright. I could move on with my life and put this all behind me. The bitterness and anger were swept away in a wave of relief. I went home, had a glass of wine on the patio and listened to some music as he sang the words to "The River" Garth Brooks' melodic voice echoed from my living room.

That was the last night I felt the peace that surpasses all understanding for a long time. The feeling that everything was going to be okay. The feeling that warms your heart, stills your fears, and releases a calming effect from your head to your toes. The feeling that your soul will no longer drown in troubled waters and no matter what happens, you will be fine.

The next day, my mom died from cancer.

Chapter 3

Cancer Thunderstorm

Two years after Mom had her stroke, she was diagnosed with stomach cancer. One day, everything was clear sailing after recovery and then *bang*. The news hit the family like a lightning bolt in a thunderstorm. Mom had Stage 4 cancer. The cancer had spread to her liver and part of her bowel. We knew she didn't have long. The tumours were so large in her stomach they blocked the passageway for her to eat. Food could not physically go down, and if she did manage to eat, everything would come right back up. I took some time off work to help take care of Mom and be with her as much as I could. I knew time was short and all the time I could spend with her was precious. I had a couple months left in my two-year notice period at work, so I took my personal leave days and some vacation days to go home. Travel was difficult for so many reasons. I had to leave Brandon and Darryl behind and make the long drive to Saskatchewan. I'm not used to driving far distances on my own. I was worried about falling asleep behind the wheel—I'd done that before—but I had to go. I never would have forgiven myself if I didn't. There is a feeling of helplessness when you are separated by a great distance from a sick and dying parent. It's a deep, lonely, gnawing feeling that eats away at your heart like the smoldering embers of a fire.

When I was a little girl, Mom used to rock me and sing songs to me. Mom didn't have the most beautiful voice, by her own account, but it sounded lovely to me. She had once described her voice as warbly, but that was harsh. Mom's voice was quiet, a little shaky, but sweet and on key. I knew when she was singing, she was singing just for me. It was a tender, complete love that only a mother has for her child. She would rock me in the living room in our 1970s floral print rocking chair. The fabric was velour with blue flowers on a light brown background. The soft, puffy chair matched perfectly with the dark brown wood wall paneling and the blue sculpted carpet. The chair springs would squeak slightly with every backward sway. I loved it and I think I was about ten years old the last time she rocked me. *Too bad a person must grow up.*

During the short time I took care of Mom during her fight with cancer, I would go into her room at night and sing to her. It was bedtime and singing lullabies brought her comfort, a way to fall asleep peacefully. Mom was pretty much bed ridden by this time. She would only come out of her room to eat what little she could and go to the bathroom. I sat on the edge of her bed and would sing melody after melody. Quietly and tenderly, like she used to sing to me so many years ago. It was my turn to deliver the peace, comfort, and love the way a daughter should love her mother. Dad would sit in the living room while I was singing. He would applaud after each song and once said, "Bravo, Char." Mom would quietly lie on her bed and listen, hanging on every note. After I ran through my complete repertoire of songs, I would kiss her on the cheek and wish her a goodnight. "Goodnight, Char," she said peacefully and would drift off to sleep. The songs were the same ones she sang to me so many years ago. Most of them were Sunday School songs but our favourite was "Little Sir Echo." I taught all these songs to my son, Brandon, when he was little and I will sing them to my grandchildren when they are born, too.

Over the four months of Mom's illness, my family and I came back for a few more visits. The last time I talked to my mom on the phone she asked, "When are you coming home, Charlotte?" There was a finality in Mom's voice. She sounded distant, like she knew I wouldn't be home to see her again. Her childlike tone tugged at my heartstrings. Mom was getting ready to go home to Heaven. She had fought long enough.

"As soon as I find out if I get a severance package or not, Mom. I have a meeting this Thursday to find out what is happening. Once I know what's up, I can come home for a visit."

"Okay." Mom's voice was quiet, reserved and tired. It seemed to be a shorter conversation than usual. There was a sense she was disappointed that I wouldn't be home sooner. Mom never liked talking on the phone. I'm not sure why, she just didn't enjoy it. And that was it. The last conversation I had with Mom.

I was running through the meadows in triumph one day, and crouching in the corner the next, trying to shield myself from the storm of Mom's death. In an instant, the walls had come crashing down around me as the winds blew and the waters rose. Freed from the constraints of a toxic work environment only to be thrown into grief over the death of my mom. It was odd, though, as I had almost mourned Mom's death when she had her stroke. I think in some ways, it made her death easier for me to deal with. Still, there was an emptiness I felt when Mom passed away. Mom was always there to call when I had questions about cooking or any funny little thing that I didn't know how to do. Mom knew everything. Now, my source was gone. She was no longer there to talk to whenever I needed her. I felt emotionally and physically drained. I did not feel alone, though. My coworkers, church family, and friends were supportive. Their kindness and generosity in gifts, hugs, and faith were what brought me through the sadness.

I would think about Mom all the time but these thoughts didn't debilitate my daily life. The world kept on turning and I know Mom would have said, "Oh, for heaven's sake, pull up your socks and get on with it." Brandon and Darryl needed me, so I focused on taking care of them. When I needed alone time, I would sit by my fishpond in the backyard and read. My coworkers bought me an angel sculpture and a calla lily to plant by my pond. While I read, I would glance up at the flower and Mom's angel. The drizzling water of the fountain and the quiet hum of my thoughts brought me peace.

I chose to spend the night of Mom's funeral out at the farm where I grew up instead of staying at Mom and Dad's apartment in the city. Darryl, Brandon, my brother Daren, and Dad were all there. I needed to go home. I needed to be where I grew up and had the most powerful memories of Mom.

The farm is quiet and feels far away from civilization, even though it's situated 16 kilometres from Waldeck, a tiny town of three hundred people in Saskatchewan. Grain fields of wheat surround the farm like a green river, the odd ripple forming from winds that blow over the small hills. All you can hear are tractors working in the fields in the distance, frogs croaking, crickets chirping, and the occasional song of the meadowlark. The odd half-ton pick-up truck might drive by causing billows of dust like a dirt cloud to sneak over the fields to the farmyard. The farmyard is spacious with buildings that surround the house at an ample distance giving plenty of room in the centre of the yard. The barn is now a faded red but still stands as a massive sentinel overlooking the yard. Towering Lombardy poplars, blue spruce, and chokecherry trees border the yard on three sides for protection from the harsh winds that belt the land in summer and winter. The trees rock back and forth in the breeze, shielding the farm from the prairie winds and storms of life. The shelter of the swaying trees remind me of how Mom used to rock me so many years ago.

There is something about music and how it stirs up emotions, good, sad, or bad. Mom loved Elvis Presley. She used to say before Elvis exploded onto the music scene that all the young girls had were singers who stood in one place and strummed their guitars like Perry Como and Gene Autry. Then Elvis showed up and *wow*. Hearing Elvis sing takes me to when Mom, Dad, Darryl, Brandon and I went to Nashville and Memphis on vacation. It takes me to times when we would dance in the basement to Elvis songs as a child. In Elvis' voice Mom would find refuge from her troubles and now it's my jewel for connecting to so many happy memories of my childhood.

Elvis' rendition of "Bridge Over Troubled Water" came over the speakers in the farmhouse living room while we were reminiscing about Mom and the funeral. Elvis' voice starts low and rich, the melody so soothing; the voice of a friend promising to take away all your tears and be there for you. When no one else is there to stand beside you, you have that one person; that one true friend who will walk with you on your journey. The song offers comfort in dark times and I was in dark times. The song promises that things will get better and your time to shine will come. Mom was now shining in Heaven with God and all the angels, and now God was comforting me through that song.

Brandon, seeing I needed a hug, came over, wrapped his arms around me and slowly danced with me while I buried my head into his fifteen-year-old chest; my remaining mascara soaking into his white shirt. My son is an incredible young man. That day he truly was my bridge over troubled water.

The time had come to leave the farm and go back to life in Alberta. Even though Mom was gone, life still had to go on. One foot had to be put in front of the other. The world did not stop turning, even if I sometimes wanted it to. The drive home was a blur. The numbing, dull feeling of life without Mom was setting in. I started having thoughts of regret that I didn't go home sooner to see her one last time. I knew I shouldn't beat myself up like that, but I couldn't help it. I kept reminding myself that a life of what-ifs was no way to live. I had to keep trying to place one foot in front of the other.

Back at work, even though I had received my severance notice, I had to fulfill my duties and complete my full two-years working notice. Severance had been offered in June and my last day would be in August. I went back to work and started going through the motions of a regular workday. My coworkers were supportive and understanding. There were many people I enjoyed working with and good friends I had made. My focus was on connecting with each and every one of the people that meant something to me over the past years of work; to say goodbye, as I prepared for a new life away from cubicle-land. It was bittersweet because I was happy to be leaving my job but I knew I would miss the people. Everyone always says they will stay in touch or come visit but they never do.

This was a time of so many goodbyes in my life.

Chapter 4

The Lowest Point

After being laid off, I decided I wanted my own business. It was time to establish new routines in my life; routines that would be effective for working at home by myself, rather than being surrounded by people all day long, dealing with constant distractions. To start the day off, I would sit outside and enjoy my breakfast. Summer is short in Canada so I took every advantage I could to enjoy the outdoors since I no longer had to get up at 5:00 a.m. to rush to work. I was on my own schedule.

I needed a break from mental labour so I took one full week to clean the house. It was a season of change so it was time to declutter and organize. This also gave me time to clear my head of the cobwebs that had accumulated over the last couple of years. I would take a break in the afternoon and go for walks with my friend, Janice, and her miniature poodle-cross, Cooper. Janice was like my mom-away-from-home. She helped me during the grieving process by always being there for me. Janice has a faith bigger and higher than the mountains and her support was exactly what I needed. It seems I had more than one bridge in my life.

Dogs are a wonderful reminder of how to live in the moment and that is exactly what I needed to do at that point in time. I didn't need to soak into my grief and let it consume me. I needed to focus on the here and now and what needed to be done to move forward. Seeing Cooper's grey, fuzzy, smiling face as I met them for afternoon walks put a smile on my face and one back into my heart. It's funny, Cooper and I have a special bond. He adores me and I adore him. I think what he really loved were the back rubs I gave him when I went over for visits. He is the funniest little dog

I have known. I shouldn't say little dog. Cooper is a wee bit overweight for a tiny dog and he is obsessed with food. His plumpness under his curly fur adds to his charm, though. Everyone smiles when they see Cooper.

After a full week of cleaning my house and refreshing my mind, it was time to get back to work. For motivation, I signed up for an early morning motivational video to put me in the right mindset. I immersed myself into listening to entrepreneurial speakers that had as much zeal to get me motivated as I did. I bought a day planner to chart out my day so I wouldn't become distracted by other things to do at home. I had to set boundaries or I knew I would get distracted. Darryl was on the same page as I was about having my own business and his support was extremely helpful.

The entrepreneurial flame had been lit in me a few years earlier so I took this time to fan the flames. My husband and I both enjoyed the world of real estate. A couple years earlier, we had purchased two homes in Austin, Texas as long-term rentals. I had recently attended a conference where they talked about buying tax deeds in the United States. It sounded like a no-brainer. The man leading the seminar was a master salesman. Literally hundreds of thousands of properties go on auction for back taxes each year in the US. Certainly, there would be some for us to buy. I purchased his course and got to work learning a new strategy for real estate, anticipating what would soon be my full-time career.

I delved into the course head-on. It was challenging and I learned a lot. But after thousands of dollars spent on the course, coaches and travelling to tax sales, we had nothing. Zero. Zilch. The properties were all useless or they were pulled from the auctions at the last minute when people came to pay their taxes. My tax auction days were over. I was certain it would work and my next career would be a full-time real estate investor. I had expected my severance would hold us over until I landed our first deal. I knew everything would be okay. I was wrong. Doing anything with the sole desire to make money only promotes negative energy, and our focus was on money and little else.

I was terrified. *What if I have to go back to a job?* I so desperately wanted the freedom of working from home and I could see my dream slipping away. I was also afraid of what others would think of me. Here I was going on this exciting new venture and it wasn't working. The naysayers would be right. I hate it when that happens. I didn't want to live the same life as I had been and go back to a regular job. But, I was starting to realize that I would have to find a job, and soon. The failure hit when we were standing in line at a checkout in Walmart and Darryl's phone rang. It was our phone provider and they wanted payment. We had fallen behind on the bills and that had never happened to us before. I felt like I had swallowed a concrete cinder block. The burden of our mistakes was crushing the life out of me.

I began to realize how quickly my severance would be eaten up. Darryl and I were simply not prepared for living on one income. More than once in the year since I became unemployed, we had anticipated money would come in and it didn't. We had maxed out our credit cards on courses about real estate investing, travelling to sales, and attending real estate conferences. Money we had planned to use to pay off debt was supposed to come from a couple of sources but didn't materialize. Darryl had changed jobs and we thought we would get a portion of his pension contributions back. But because he had worked for the company for seventeen years, his pension was vested and we would receive nothing as it was all to go into a Locked in Retirement Account— we couldn't touch it. We were sure we would get a property to sell at the tax auctions and that didn't happen either. Darryl was also supposed to get a large income tax refund but the Canada Revenue Agency declined his expense claims and would not refund any money for that tax year. The CRA was not done with us yet.

Now, six months into my unemployment, we were in trouble. Big trouble. The nail was hammered into the coffin on the day we got a tax notice from the CRA stating we owed $18,000. Darryl leaned against the wall and tears came to his eyes as he listened while I read the income tax return results.

"Don't worry. We will figure out a way to deal with this. We always do." I tried to offer comforting words but inside I was alarmed. I had no idea what we were going to do. I felt like a failure and I was scared that everyone would find out what losers we were. We had put on a brave face like everything was wonderful but it wasn't. We so desperately wanted to be a success story. The story was not panning out the way we had foreseen it. The lump in my throat was choking me. All I could do was hug Darryl while the fear of the future gnawed away at my brain.

Everything was spiraling out of control. Neither of us had been in a situation like this before. We couldn't pay our bills. We couldn't even afford to buy food some weeks. Good thing I am a creative cook because meals got interesting. I would open the door to the pantry and see what I could possibly put together. Making creative meals for my family is a passion of mine. Rarely would you see the same meal on the table twice. It killed me that I couldn't prepare special dishes for them. The joy of going to a grocery store was gone. Yes, I loved grocery shopping. Now, a can of beans on toast was the delicacy placed before us. Thankfully, Brandon was away working for the summer. I would have been so ashamed if he were home and he noticed I couldn't buy groceries. It was one thing for Darryl and I, but the thought of putting Brandon through that experience was disconcerting. I wanted to forget this nightmare was happening. So much so that I shoved those sad little meals out of the door of my memories because they are too painful and embarrassing to recall.

People were phoning us for money so we quit answering the phone. We went to the bank and tried to get one month of our mortgage put on the end of our term to give us a small reprieve. Just one month was all we needed to catch up. The bank denied the request.

We were stuck. There was nowhere else to turn. We had been terrible money managers. I have heard you should stop chasing money because it is too fast and you will never catch it. This is true. We had become obsessed with money. It became our god and we didn't even realize it. Everything was going wrong. Darryl's health suffered due to the stress. He ended up in emergency with chest pains. I was at my wits end. I had been looking for work but the economy was in a downturn and I was not getting any phone calls for interviews. We could sell our house but we still needed somewhere to live. We could sell our properties in Texas but they were at least bringing in a little money. It just seemed there was no way out.

A last resort thought entered my mind. *What can we do that is legal to get money?* I was about to make a big mistake that would haunt me. Like a wild animal that is cornered, I was going to try anything to bring us relief from our dismal state of affairs. I didn't like my last resort thought but I just didn't know what else to do. *Maybe we could borrow some money from Dad.*

This was a new low in my life. Here I was, forty years old and I was going to ask my dad for money. Dad was not a generous person. He was not the type to give away money or donate to causes. He worked hard for his money and it was his. No one else was entitled to it. If he thought you put too much money in the offering plate at church, he would tell you so.

I had not asked my parents for so much as $20 since I was sixteen years old and had my own job. Even considering asking for a hand-out from my dad made me feel like a low life. *How could this be happening to me now? I should have it all—right?* Well, I didn't. I didn't even have self-respect anymore.

We went back to Saskatchewan to visit Dad. I was dreading this visit. *How do I ask my father for money?* We were sitting around the table talking on the first night of our visit.

Before we could even begin the awkward request Dad said, "You know, it isn't right you didn't get anything when we moved out of the house and into the apartment. You should have got something."

"That's okay Dad, don't worry about it. I wasn't there to help you and Mom move out so that's how it goes. It's okay, really."

"No, it's not." Clearly, Dad was concerned about this, even though I was not. "You should get something. Can I give you some money? God has been putting it on my heart to give you some money."

What? I didn't know what to say. Could this conversation be happening? Here I was, going to ask Dad for some money, and he was offering it. Dad just didn't offer money.

"Um. Okay. Can you take it off my inheritance?"

"No. I can't do that," he replied. I don't know why he couldn't or if he just didn't want to. When Dad gets an idea in his head, it is impossible to get it out. The conversation was surreal and awkward. I felt hollow inside. Like I had nothing left. Dad offered an amount and I said okay. I felt cornered and sick, like an animal with nowhere to turn. This was the last conversation I had imagined myself having with anyone. I had hit the lowest part of my human existence. I was taking a handout.

The next day, Dad went to the bank and gave me a cheque. I thought I would feel relief that we now had money to pay back the CRA and get a breather from the bills. I didn't feel relief though. I was an empty shell with no feeling, no emotion at all.

"Thanks Dad," I said sheepishly as he handed me the cheque. I strained a smile because Dad wanted to help us.

"You are welcome, Charlotte." Dad smiled at me and patted me on the shoulder.

I didn't feel grateful. I was disgusted with myself and how I had let myself get into this situation. This was my rock bottom. Never in my life did I picture having to ask my father for money when I was a married, grown woman with a son of my own. I was smart. I had always succeeded in everything I did. I was at the top of my class in school. When I was an employee, I had excellent performance appraisals. I had always achieved what I wanted before this period in my life. My life was supposed to be full of nice things, a big, beautiful house, nice cars, expensive clothes, and vacations whenever and wherever we wanted. At this stage in our lives, Darryl and I should have had savings in the bank, no bad debt, and wanting for nothing. We should have been in a position to help other people, not going to people for help.

With cheque in hand, and a heavy cloak of self-pity over us, we headed back to Calgary.

Chapter 5

Camp Kuriakos

Even with the loan from Dad, we were still not out of the woods. Our previous two-income quality of living now felt like a distant dream. No longer could I buy whatever I wanted at the grocery store, for example. Gourmet items were out of reach; it was all about the no-name products now. Steak became ground beef and only if it was on sale. Store flyers were my best friend and they guided my menu plans. My hair got longer because a haircut was not going to feed me, nor would it pay the bills. After all, I could put my hair up if it got unruly. The clothes in my closet were not being replenished on a regular basis. Gone were the days of shopping and buying whatever outfit I fell in love with. But in the midst of this dismal time, something happened that lit a spark of hope in our hearts.

My friend, Barb, came to me with a proposition. "Camp Kuriakos is looking for an Office Manager and I thought of you. Are you interested?" Talk about falling out of the blue. I had hoped to find employment in Sylvan Lake rather than Red Deer to avoid the half hour drive to work every day.

"Sure. I would be interested," I stated calmly. Barb put me in contact with the Camp Director, Art. Our church always had our annual Christmas party at the camp and I enjoyed the setting in the woods. There was a sense of serenity at camp. I had hoped to tap into this positive atmosphere of faith, especially after all we had been through. I drove out to the camp for the interview. Art hired me on the spot. I am a true believer that everything happens for a reason; there is no such thing as serendipity. God's hand was at work in our lives.

The camp family welcomed me and my family with open arms. Set on Sylvan Lake, the camp's rustic buildings were built as a Lutheran Bible camp to proclaim the Gospel of Christ, encourage, disciple, and build a sense of community for all people. Kuriakos was established in 1930 as a place for people to recharge, refresh and have an abundant life. God speaks in this place both through the people and through nature.

The Kuriakos Centre is the main building and it includes a kitchen, dorm rooms, and dining area. There are rustic cabins on the hill surrounded by trees that turn fire engine red and burnt orange in the fall. And by rustic, I mean rustic. There is no heat nor bathroom in these cabins equipped with bunkbeds for the adventurous camper. The chapel is at the centre of camp and has a musty, old-building smell from years gone by. Dana Lodge underwent major renovations in the fall when I began working at camp. The buildings at camp all have a woodsy, log cabin look. There are areas set apart for outdoor activities including a high-ropes course and a soccer field.

My favourite areas at camp were lakeside and up the hill where there was a covered wagon and a fire pit area with a couple of wooden benches. I would go out for a walk every day after eating lunch and stop in these two areas to meditate and pray. The peace of the trees swaying around me and the blue sky above gave me respite from my anxieties.

This environment was perfect for me after all I had been through. Kuriakos is a Greek word meaning "belonging to the Lord" and the name fits the bill. Both seasons are so different at the camp. Winter is silent, except for the deep moaning of the ice as is expands and retracts. The sound weaves its way through the forest as if spirits have come alive inside the trees. Summer is vibrant and alive with the sounds of families and children enjoying activities.

The camp setting was a new one for me. My office was an on-site mobile home shared with Art, Paul and Sarah. Paul and Sarah were busy planning camp activities while my job was mainly bookkeeping and payroll. My desk was located in what would have been a living room. This was a culture shock in itself after coming from healthcare and working in a corporate office building. Camp is humble, as it should be. The floor would need constant sweeping as the mud trekked in from campers and workers would get stuck under my chair wheels and make a gravelly sound every time I rolled. Washing the floor was required once a week. Add minor housekeeping duties to job description, please.

Camp is non-profit so the wage was meager, almost half of what I was making while in healthcare. Because of the lower wage, it was hard to get people that were qualified for administrative duties. Some areas had been considered not important so I made sure to organize the filing cabinets and keep a tight ship. Maybe no other people in camp had deadlines, but I did. It was imperative that staff be paid on time.

Being in a rural setting 18 kilometres from Sylvan Lake had its challenges. The photocopier broke down constantly and the internet was sketchy. Quite a change from having an IT Help Desk to call and come fix anything, even if their first question was always, "Did you try turning off your computer?"

Sometimes my role required me to be a den mother. Word had it that the counsellors were going to compete to see who would win the coveted title of "Charlotte's Favourite Child" that summer. I must admit, there were perks I loved, like fresh-brewed Americano's when an afternoon felt particularly long. A plate of cookies hot from the oven delivered by a smiling child and a note saying, "Thanks for all you do," can turn a broken photocopier and no Wi-Fi into secondary concerns. Being a counsellor at camp can be extremely stressful so my shoulder had a tear or two shed on it. Not to mention hugs when a determined child pushed way too many buttons and nerves were frayed.

Brandon put many volunteer hours in at Kuriakos and was hired on for the camping season three years in a row. The experience of camp and the people who work and go there transformed my family and I am eternally grateful. Brandon blossomed as a camp counsellor. From a shy, quiet boy, Brandon emerged as an energetic, outgoing entertainer of the masses at campfire, singing and role-playing the most outlandish characters. It was a delight to witness him working with the children. Brandon loved kids and being an only child he never had the chance to be a big brother. His chance to take on a leadership role was in full force at camp. One of his campers went from crying through the night for his parents to crying and clutching Brandon on the last day. Sobbing, he pleaded to Brandon, "Please, please be my counsellor next year."

My greatest joy that summer was to see Brandon grow into a deep-rooted faith. He was becoming a strong, young person with the confidence to make decisions and act on his dreams. Camp teaches leadership skills and I saw qualities come out in Brandon I didn't know were possible. Brandon seemed unscathed after all we had been through. It gave me peace to know our mistakes did not harm his character or cause him to lash out. He would be okay and that was all we could ask for.

Chapter 6

Back to School

While I was working at Camp Kuriakos, Darryl took a new job that promised much but delivered little. The position was supposed to be Central Alberta based but it ended up being based in Calgary. Darryl was driving to Calgary from Sylvan Lake four days a week. That's over 300 kilometres a day along a dangerous highway, not to mention the wear and tear this was causing on our car. Over three hours a day driving in the car to and from work was too taxing. Imagine yourself driving, all alone, over a vast plain that stretches from horizon to horizon almost every day. It was exhausting for us all, so we made the decision to move to Calgary in the fall of 2016.

My entrepreneurial spirit was still growing within, despite all the setbacks and failure we had endured. I had been doing some research as to what kind of business I could do from home. For the last twenty years, I had been working in an office, except for my hiatus after being laid off. I wanted desperately to have my own business. To no longer drive to an office or sit in a cubicle again was constantly on my mind. My dream was to never answer to a boss again, never lay in bed at night wondering if it was time for the alarm to go off yet, or never have to drive in the craziness of morning traffic to be at work on time, only to turn around at the end of the day and weave through traffic again to get back home. I didn't want to pack lunches anymore or to be told when I had to be at work and when I could take my coveted holidays. Those were experiences I wanted to remain in my past. I longed for freedom to come and go as I pleased. I wanted to build my own dream, not to build someone else's.

What could I do that I would love and be able to make money at? I love being outside, I love to travel, I love to cook and I love to take pictures. I honestly couldn't see myself cooking all day long and I had no desire to open my own restaurant. *What about a business in travel?* Maybe I could start my own travel agency and work from home. I came across the Travel & Tourism diploma program at SAIT in Calgary, so I decided to enroll. *Why not start all over again since we are moving anyway?* I applied and was put on the waiting list as the program was full.

The thought of being a travel agent had crossed my mind years earlier, but I didn't want to make minimum wage. The thought of starting over was beneath me. I was making an excellent wage and had six weeks of holidays and a pension with the health region. Ah, the crutch that keeps everyone a slave to the grind; vacation and pension. "I hate my job, but I won't give up my four weeks of holidays." If only I had a dollar each time I heard someone say that. Isn't it kind of ridiculous to be miserable for forty-eight weeks of the year only to live for the four weeks you long for? Something is wrong with this picture.

Being laid off was a reality check. Nobody was going to pay me what I was making at the health region and no one could match the benefits they offered. If I wanted a change, I had to do something extreme. Going back to school at age forty-two was a drastic change for me. It's a frightening thought, going back to school as an adult. *How could I compare to the young people with so much technical advantage?* I was determined that if I got accepted, I was going to rock it. My heart and soul would be poured into the two-year diploma program. After all, travel was now going to be my life. I had no connections in the industry so going back to school was a way to give myself credibility in the world of travel.

Just before we moved, we were financially forced to sell our rental properties in Texas. There was an unforeseen increase in property taxes reducing the monthly cash flow to the negative. We could no longer afford to keep the houses as we would be sending money to pay the taxes. The houses were supposed to be our retirement plan but it wasn't working out that way. We were still just squeaking by after the rug had been ripped out from under us with my layoff. Equity rich but cash poor—that was us. So, we put them on the market and they both sold within three days. God bless Texas.

The call came a week before we were set to move to Calgary. I had been accepted into the program at SAIT.

"Darryl, guess what? You are married to a schoolgirl!" I messaged to Darryl.

"That's nice." *Well, that was a boring response,* I thought. He clearly didn't get it. At the very least he could have thought I was getting into something kinky and sent me an emoji with hearts in the eyes. When Darryl was at work, he was in a different zone. When off work, he was playful, responsive, gentle, and caring. While at work, however, I would often get his "inside work voice" answers when I'd call him or send a message. There was one time I called him at work and told him my leg hurt. "Why don't you go punch yourself in the face and you'll forget about the pain in your leg." Whoa, that was the wrong response and a very abrupt end to our conversation. Dumbfounded, I told my coworkers at the health region about his rude remark. They thought it was hilarious. I, at the time, did not.

Note to Self: Don't call Darryl at work and expect a heart-felt reply.

So, I had to spell out my schoolgirl remark for him and let him know I was going back to school. "Oh! That's wonderful!" was the response I got now that I was not being coy. That was the reaction I was looking for. The only thing left to fall into place was the sale of our house in Sylvan Lake. Surely, it would sell quickly. It was a nice house and we loved it. There had to be someone out there who felt the same way about our home.

August was ending and it was time to move. The end of September long weekend means back to school. The house had not sold yet so we packed up and left it vacant, positive it would sell before winter began. We were beginning to develop a habit of being certain of things that don't come to fruition. The only certainty is whatever you expect will happen, will not happen. But now everything should be okay—with the sale of our houses in Texas, we had a cushion to cover our bills while I went back to school full time. Darryl's new job would be great and all would be right in the world. Life was going to be grand.

Chapter 7

A Schoolgirl in Greece

The first day of school was a little nerve wracking. I honestly didn't expect to make any friends. I was going to school to learn and work. I had no time for frivolities. Walking into the college classroom, I saw two older guys sitting together. I sat next to Shawn, a balding forty-three-year-old man, whom I had met at orientation. The classroom had long tables with five big rolling chairs at each table. It was bright with huge windows and a million-dollar view of the city of Calgary and the mountains.

Shawn appeared to be a father-figure type. He looked serious and I thought if he was back in school, then he was going to be as serious about his studies as I was.

"Hi, I'm Drew," said the tall blonde drink of water sitting next to Shawn.

"Nice to meet you, Drew. I'm Charlotte."

Drew was in his early twenties and seemed chipper and happy to be back in school. He was polite and had a good sense of humour.

"Well, Charlotte, looks like you and I will have to be the parents in the class and keep everyone in line." Shawn was a year older than me. It was a relief to not be the only person in the class over the age of thirty. I could tell everything was going to be okay.

The room filled up with bright-eyed, excited young people. All eager to get to know new friends and begin a new chapter in their lives. It's interesting how certain people just click. Danny, the campus hottie, sat in front of Shawn, Drew and me. Sara, a feisty redhead who would become my college-friend-forever, sat in the front row on the other side of the room. She was older than that just-outta-high-school type too. The five of us sat together on our first break and the rest of the semester we were inseparable, killing it on projects and quickly becoming known as "The Fab Five." We were five dedicated and highly driven individuals. We worked so well together and had an unbeatable synergy. The first semester was my favourite time at SAIT. Sadly, the next semester broke the five of us up. I was put in a group without any of them. Danny and Sara were together in another group. Drew and Shawn in yet another. I was devastated.

Even though my world seemed over—how quickly we revert to the high school mentality—I was bound and determined to survive the class I had been put into. My determination didn't last long. After a week of misery, I switched with another student to be in the same classes as Danny and Sara. I was paying to go to school and to spend the rest of my time in a class of people I had nothing in common with just wouldn't fly. I needed to be with my peeps.

Year one finished and then it was time to take the SAIT study tour. I was ecstatic when I found out where the trip was going to be—Greece was on my bucket list. Historical sites are a passion of mine and Greece is not lacking in this regard. All my life I had dreamed of seeing the Acropolis. I have a yearning to see places with such historic significance before they disappear forever. Walking in the same place as historical figures and trying to picture how they lived fuels my imagination, not to mention takes my breath away. Growing up, I was fascinated with Greek mythology to the point of wishing I could have my own herd of winged horses.

I could write an entire book about that two-week experience in Greece with forty twenty-something SAIT students whose number one priority was to get drunk. Okay, not all of them felt that way but a heavy portion swayed to that side. I thanked God daily for Sara who was along with me on the trip or I may have killed someone. Sara is a fiercely independent woman and had travelled to many countries all by herself, so a bus tour of more than forty people was not her cup of tea. We kept each other sane.

Sara hated the bus and being stuck on it for so many miles. Our tour guide would come over the loudspeaker to give us the itinerary. Because this was a study tour for school, the itinerary was exhausting. We were rushed from site to site and hotel to hotel. Not what Sara was used to.

"Sara, you are furrowing your brow," I said to her with a smirk. Sara was going to blow a cog if she had to spend more time on the bus, and here our guide was telling us that was exactly how most of the day was going to be. I had to laugh at Sara and point out her obvious pain. Her brow tightened up even more behind her sunglasses.

"Stop it, Sara. You are going to get wrinkles."

"Ugh. I know." Sara took her index finger and rubbed between her eyebrows ferociously. "I can't stand it. I'm going to throat punch someone if I don't get off this bus."

"You know, I saw a German Shepherd about five miles back while you were sleeping." Sara burst out laughing. This became a private joke between us because most of the people on the tour were obsessed with the cats in Greece. "Oh! Look at the kitty! Oh! Look at the cat! Oh! Aren't they cute!" They were mongrels, stray cats that were full of disease and I couldn't understand why someone would want to touch a cat that was covered in saliva and looked half dead. *They are cats, people. We have cats in Canada. Big. Hairy. Deal.*

*Note to Self: When crammed into a tour bus with
millennials pumped up with raging hormones and last
night's booze fest, keep a level-headed friend close at hand.
And don't forget a bottle of wine for later.*

"Let's play a game to get to know each other better." *Thanks,
Mr. Tour Guide Tom, but we already know each other enough.* Of
course, some of the young ones were tickled to go to the front of
the bus and talk about themselves. Tom was an excellent guide
and deserved a medal for the things he put up with; young
women hitting on him, carrying drunk people up hillsides after a
night out in Delphi, people crying because they had no friends.
Tom never batted an eye and took it all in stride, making everyone
feel welcome and loved as a friend.

"Each of you give us three statements about yourselves and
one of them is going to be a lie. We have to guess which one." Tom
was laying down the ground rules.

The blonde bombshell in the group stood up and talked into
the microphone. "Hi. My name is Khloe." *Honestly, I don't
remember the first two things she said.* The last remark left an
impact, on Sara in particular. "This is my real hair colour." From
near the back of the bus, Sara shot her hand up in the air, finger
pointed directly at Khloe and yelled out, "Girl. That isn't even
your real hair." You see, Sara was a hair stylist and it was obvious
to her that Khloe was wearing extensions. And now, everyone else
knew Khloe's secret. The bus had got the best of Sara. She just
couldn't help herself and as soon as she blew Khloe's platinum
blonde cover, she was sorry. The rest of the bus burst out in
laughter. Khloe was furious. *That was her problem. She walked right
into it.*

*Note to Self: Take along medications to knock
you out if you need a break from the masses.*

Besides history, my other favourite part of travel is food. Greece is my favourite food destination. Greek food in Canada is just not the same as the food in Greece. I have never had potatoes taste as good as they do in Greece. I have heard it is a special potato they grow on one of the islands. The potatoes are so tasty because of the rich, volcanic soil they grow in. When you bite into a potato prepared in Greece, it will melt in your mouth without being mushy. Olive oil, lemon and light herbs enhance the flavour giving the potato a rich, creamy, buttery taste and feel. And the baklava. *Oh, the baklava.* Tender filo pastry soaked in honey and lemon, brimming with walnuts and cinnamon. But I am getting ahead of myself. Baklava is dessert. The feta cheese is fresh, creamy, not too salty, and comes in a big chunk on your Greek salad, not as overly-brined crumbles of chalk. The hummus is to die for. Fresh hummus with buttery olive oil, a hint of garlic, and a smoothness like silk, pairs perfectly with fresh pita bread. *Take me back for the food, please.*

I learned so much about myself on that school trip. I learned that large-group bus tours are not for me. I have done a small-group tour with nine people and that was enjoyable. My favourite travel companions are my husband and son. I like the freedom and independence of planning my own activities and not being restricted to the itinerary and actions of forty other people.

Chapter 8

The Ring

After Greece and summer was over, it was back to school for the second and final year of travel and tourism studies. I was excited to get back to it and put a business plan in place. I planned to get guidance and direction from my instructors and from other travel industry professionals.

I talked to a person who worked for a travel agency in the corporate travel division. Most of the work was spent staring at and analyzing spreadsheets, booking flights and hotels for corporate travellers. No thanks. I didn't want to sit behind a desk anymore. *Was I now back to square one? What could I do to combine travel and my talents?* My goal was to get out from behind a desk and a nine to five regime, not pour myself full fledge back into the grind. I yearned for freedom to choose my work and my schedule. I imagined myself as my own boss. Setting my day out the way I wanted to spend it. There would be travel, but there would be a lot of hard work too. I knew my own business wouldn't be a cake walk. Rather than sitting at a desk, I imagined myself out meeting people at networking events. Building connections with people is so important to success. I imagined planning people's perfect getaway and delivering a unique experience made just for them based on my own journeys. I wanted to create something special, something unique that would make a person want to travel more or to finally take that dream vacation they had been putting on the back burner.

Destinations at SAIT is the live travel agency run by students on campus. It is an excellent environment for students to see how a travel agency operates and what a travel agent does. The course itself is not solely geared toward being a travel agent but it does expose you to this element. Travel agents offer value to their customers, especially if something goes wrong on the trip. They are your first point of contact if something goes awry with your flight or any part of your booking. Have you been told your flight is overbooked and you will not be getting to your next destination? Well, if you booked through a travel agent, they can help negotiate with the airlines for you. They know the traveller's rights.

During second year, all students are given two separate shifts in the agency for credit in the course. On the first day, our instructor, Stephanie, asked everyone in the room what they wanted to do.

"I want to be a travel writer." *Where did that come from? Did I just say that? Don't be ridiculous, Charlotte. How in the world are you going to get started as a writer? Will anyone read my work? Will it ever make money? Do I have a deep-seeded desire to be poor for the rest of my life?* But now, now I said it out loud and that made it real. Saying it aloud felt good. *Yeah, I'm gonna be a travel writer.* I had been doing some research on how to become a travel blogger and writer. When I was in high school, I liked to write essays. The research on the topic and the editing process was always fascinating and a challenge for me. I could be a travel writer and work from anywhere in the world. *Bingo.*

A few weeks later, we went on a field trip to Air Canada. Darryl picked me up and we gave my instructor, Stephanie, a ride back to SAIT. "You know, Charlotte, in all the years I've been teaching, you are the only one who said they wanted to be a travel writer."

"Really?"

"Yes, have you heard of Pete and Dalene Heck of Hecktic Travels? They left everything and travelled the world. They blog about it and they are the sweetest couple. They have made a successful business out of it too."

"No, I haven't heard about them. That sounds exactly like what I want to do." I had to learn more about the Hecks and what they went through to change their lives. *What was their business model like? How did they survive a life of travel without eating ichiban every day?* I planned to go home and find out everything I could about this intriguing couple and their business.

It turns out the Hecks used housesitting as their travel niche. They had gone through turbulent times and needed to make changes in their lives too. I connected with their story. *If they could sell everything and go from country to county housesitting and make a business out of it, why couldn't I?*

But would that lifestyle work for us? Could we afford to do it? Could we afford not to do it? Maybe I'm too much of a dreamer and expect to have my cake and eat it too. I was worried that if I went down the writing path, we would end up broke again and I vowed to never go down that road again. We had big plans before for businesses that didn't work out. *Would this one fail too? No — I didn't go back to school to go and get a job and fall into the status quo.* I wanted to do something different; if someone wants to live an extraordinary life, they need to live differently. And there it was. My course was set. *Travel writing.* Now I had to figure out how to make it happen.

Darryl and I made the decision to follow my writing dreams. Upon graduating from SAIT, we would travel to launch my writing career. After all, you must travel in order to write about it. The only thing standing in our way was our house in Sylvan Lake; after a year and a half on the market, it still had not sold.

Central Alberta had been hit hard by the recession and houses were simply not moving. All this time, we had been paying double everything. Rent at one, mortgage at the other, utilities, insurance... The sale of our houses in Texas helped us keep on top of the bills, but this was getting old. To top it off, the engine on our car was finished so we were also making a car payment on a vehicle we couldn't even drive. It was past warranty so the car company wouldn't do anything to help us. That's $15,000 owing on a useless vehicle. Oh yeah, we had also just put new tires on it a month before it gave up the ghost.

One cold night in December, I pulled up to our house. I looked at my phone and there was an email from our realtor. We had an offer on the house. I felt I had the renewed hope of a lame man that had just been told to rise and walk. Relief washed over me. *We would finally be free.* Tears of joy poured down my face. I couldn't believe it. A year and half of waiting and praying was over. The offer was less than we hoped for but that was okay. We just needed it to be gone so we could move forward.

Now with the house sold, we could continue with our plans to travel. We had no credit card debt and no mortgage. We could make this work as we would have virtually no major monthly bills to pay. It was time to begin planning our journey.

April 20, 2018 was my last day of school. Darryl hated his job so he quit. Life is too short to be miserable. We felt this was a "now or never" situation in our lives. Our son was going to be working at Camp Kuriakos again starting in the spring so he would be fed, housed and watered while we were away. He was twenty years old now, about time for him to spread his wings and fly, too. We had hoped our time away from Canada would also encourage him to make some decisions on what he wanted to do with his life. We never forced him to go to school. Neither of us believe imposing school is an effective way to grow, not to mention the complete waste of money if the child is not ready and does not know what they want to do. *Who knows what they want to be when they grow up anyway?*

As I headed for my last train ride away from school using the Calgary transit system I despised, I reflected on the two years of school, what I had learned, and the people I had met. It was a forty-five minute ride from SAIT to the station where Darryl would be pick me up for the last time—thankfully. I hated riding the train. I still do. Matt, who was in my classes the last year of school, was sleeping on the seat next to me. Matt was a good-looking guy in his mid-twenties with dark hair and a six o'clock shadow. We usually rode the train together, as he got off at the same stop. I'd love to say he was great company on the dreaded ride but I swear Matt has narcolepsy—he slept most of the way there. I know if I didn't wake him up, he would end up back at SAIT. Let's put it this way, Matt is a guy who can fall asleep standing up in a museum in Delphi, Greece and also while waiting at red lights. I am not sure how he even has a license. His heart is in the right place, though. Matt is one of those guys in an adult body but remains a kid at heart. He gets along with everyone and is a friend that is always up for a cold beer and good times. His favourite attire was a blow-up Tyrannosaurus Rex suit that he wore to class one day. He also would attest that a onesie is essential apparel for watching TV.

My phone buzzed. I couldn't believe what I was seeing on the little screen in front of me. My brother, Daren, had texted, "Is this what I think it is?" In the picture was a ring. A gold ring with six coloured stones embedded in the band. It was my Grandmother's family ring. A ring we all thought was lost forever. When I was seven months pregnant, Mom had promised I could have

Grandma's family ring. I had worn it at my wedding as "something old."

"I'll put it away in a safe place for you," Mom had said. After Mom's death, our family searched high and low for this ring in vain. Nowhere to be found, we gave up on it, certain she had given it to someone else. Now, here it was, staring up at me from my phone with a note inside the box, "To Charlotte From Mom and Grandma xxoo Sept 97." It had been so long since I had seen Mom's handwriting. There is a personal, heartfelt touch when someone handwrites a note. Handwriting is like a fingerprint, so unique. I had kept a box of parchment paper where Mom had written my name on the side of it so I could have a sample of her handwriting. I knew she would never write again. But I did see her handwriting again—and it was on a note she had written to me over twenty years ago.

Emotions began to take over. My phone was shaking in my hand, my heart was speeding up, and a lump welled up in my throat. *Don't cry. Don't cry. Don't cry. Matt is sitting beside me and he'll freak out if he wakes up and sees you bawling like a baby. Control yourself, woman. Breathe. Breathe. Breathe. Okay.* I'd be okay until I got to the parking lot where Darryl would pick me up. Then— Niagara Falls.

The train pulled into the station and Matt and I parted ways. As soon as he was out of sight, I let the waterworks go. Some women love to cry. They set aside time in their schedule for it. I do not. Crying is so draining and I look hideous when I cry. The blubbering and contorted face is not becoming, and talking is out of the question.

There I stood, bawling my eyes out on the sidewalk waiting for my ride. Darryl pulled up and I jumped in the car, anxious to get out of the public eye. "I'm okay. I'm okay. These are happy tears," I sobbed.

"What's going on?" Darryl looked so confused. He thought I'd be smiling when he picked me up today. School was *done*. I showed him the picture on my phone.

"It's Mom's ring. Daren found it in her junk jewelry drawer. He almost threw it out when he was cleaning up some of her stuff." I still couldn't believe he had found it, and on this day of all days. To me, it was like Mom was saying, "You go, Charlotte. Go on your trip. Everything will be okay."

Note to Self: Mom's love never leaves. She will always be looking out for me. Always.

Almost a week later, I stood on the highest hill in the rural municipality where I grew up, overlooking my childhood farm, wrapped in a golden sunset. The sky was dancing in its radiant colours, drawing out the yellow hues of the stubble fields. Mom's presence is on the hill. I snapped a picture to capture the moment. It is my favourite picture from 2018, not just because of the incredible sunset, but because of where it was taken—Mom's hill.

I needed to go back home to connect with my roots. My father's health and mind were failing with age. I wondered if he would remember us when we got back. It seemed Dad's dementia was progressing rapidly. It was essential to go back home to see him before we left. We made a quick weekend trip back to Saskatchewan. There is always something special about going home.

Going home also helps me feel closer to Mom. We always stay at the farm where I grew up. I have a sense of peace when I am there. Partly because there is no traffic and no dreaded public transit system.

The farm is my anchor, my constant attachment to the days back when I was a little girl dreaming about travel and what was beyond the vast fields of the prairies. The farm has an eternal feeling to it. No matter where I go, or what I do, the farm will always be there to welcome me back.

Chapter 9

Texas

Europe was going to be a big part of our travels. Darryl had family in Belgium and I had always wanted to meet them. We would be sure to spend time with them. What other destinations had I always wanted to go to? Egypt, the Holy Land, Germany… those were tops on my list. It was a little petrifying and dreamlike that we were going to do this trip. We were about to say goodbye to Canada for almost six months. I couldn't wait. Before this trip, the longest I had been away from home was two weeks.

We love Texas so we decided we would start our quest in the Lone Star State. Darryl was going to use this time to get his real estate investing business going again. Texas was our state of choice to invest in, with Austin being our focus. We felt being there for a month would help us get some momentum. We had also considered buying a winter home in the area to escape the clenches of our Canadian winters. The older we get, the harder the winters get. *Would we love Texas as much after being there for a month?* No time like the present to find out.

Friends of ours had just converted one of their houses into an Airbnb. They gave us a smashing deal to stay for the month of May. Things were starting to pan out. On May 1st, we flew to Austin to stay for the month. Darryl, to kick-start his real estate career, and me, to begin discovering what my niche would be for my blog. According to the experts, a niche is essential in creating a successful blog. I knew what I loved about travel so now to narrow it down to a feasible idea. It was time to develop my talents.

I don't know why, but I have always had this bizarre fear of being turned away from a country at the border, crushing all my travel dreams. Here we were at the airport in Calgary, ready to proceed through customs for our month-long stay in Texas. *What do we say? Do we tell them our trip is for real estate? For my travel blog?* I have learned to only answer customs with simple answers, which pretty much means "yes" or "no" and one-word replies. No need to blather on about what they are not asking about.

"Where are you headed today, ma'am?" The customs officer clearly had a Southern accent.

"Austin, Texas."

"Have you tried Franklin's barbeque?"

"No, we haven't," I said, waiting for more official questions to come next. He opened our passports and looked at the pictures.

"Well, you better get there early 'cause there is always a line-up. Enjoy the barbeque." He handed our passports back to us and waved us by. *That was it?* I guess we've been to Texas so many times they just don't care anymore. *Yeehaw!*

It was early in the morning and we had a bit of time since customs and security were such a breeze, so we stopped for breakfast.

"Can you believe we are actually doing this, Darryl?" I couldn't stop smiling since passing through customs.

"No, but it's awesome." Darryl had a radiant glow of excitement and anticipation on his face. He looked like an enthusiastic schoolboy on his first trip to a football game. He gets the same look when he's ready to bite into a juicy burger at his favourite restaurant. As we sat and sipped our coffees we drank in the moment, knowing what we were about to embark on. I sent our executive coach, Mark, a message. "We are at YYC and ready to head to AUS!" Using the airport acronyms for Calgary, Alberta and Austin, Texas made it feel so official that we were legitimate travellers now.

"And so it begins," he messaged back. "Enjoy the process."

The process. Ah, yes. The process. Mark leads a mastermind group that we are a part of and the process is everything. We were going through a brainstorming activity about what kind of travel business I should start when he came up with the suggestion that we take off and travel. I had returned from the Greece study tour the night before so I was operating in a mind fog. "Sounds like Charlotte needs to go on a six-month exploration trip," he said with a black sharpie in his hand while standing in our media room. An easel of paper in front of him with writing all over it of ideas the group had shouted out. Just go. Explore this big old world. Discover what we loved about travel and then decide what type of niche or business would suit my personality. *Could we really do that? Could we become one of those people who forget everything and roam?* I have always had a deep sense of admiration for people that left on an extended trip or took a mission somewhere. *Would we be one of those people?* Mark is excellent at coming up with creative ideas for change. He isn't afraid to challenge anyone to examine their limiting beliefs. Mark lifted the fog and shone a big old spotlight on a new idea.

We knew this would change our lives and change who we were. We were ready. After five years of extreme stress from sicknesses, death, layoffs, financial chaos and a detested job, we were ready to transform into new people. I have always been a high-strung person with little patience. I wanted things now and they had to be perfect. Perfectionism is a killer. Nothing is ever perfect. Nothing. And nothing ever turns out as we plan. I was excited to see where the process would lead us.

******

It was dark when we arrived at our new month-long home in Round Rock, a suburb of Austin. We opened the door to find soft music playing, a bottle of wine in the kitchen, pimento cheese and crackers in the fridge, and farm-fresh eggs on their way in the morning. The warm, welcoming environment was easy to settle into. We wanted to see what it was like to live in Texas so our weekdays would be spent working on our businesses. The weekends would be designated for exploration of new areas. I would be building Darryl's website as well as working on my own. We took the next day to settle in and relax and then it was time to hit the ground running.

First things first. Barbeque. Whenever we go to Texas one of the first things we always do is go for barbeque. There are places in Canada claiming "authentic Texas barbeque." I tell you…they lie. You have not had authentic Texas barbeque unless you have eaten it in Texas. Southern barbeque techniques put our barbeque in Canada to shame. The smoking, sauces and rubs are out of this world. You can smell their smoke pits from miles away. As soon as you step out of the car, you should be able to smell the delectable aroma. My mouth is already starting to water. We have our favourites and I know there are more incredible places to discover. Brisket and ribs that melt in your mouth. Oh, and I'll have a side of creamy coleslaw and potato salad. Don't forget the fresh baked bread with whipped honey butter that dissolves on the surface like hot sunshine into the sea. Add a side of pickles and onions and you know all is good in the world.

We were in Texas over Mother's Day. This would be my first Mother's Day away from Brandon, which saddened me. He is our only child and I adore him. Being a mother has been the best vocation in the world. We wanted more children but God chose to bless us with only one. Nobody could tell us why I was unable to conceive again. It just wasn't meant to be. It took me nearly a decade of trying to get pregnant again to finally accept Brandon was going to be our single gift. I came from a family where the women got pregnant when they said the word, so they didn't understand, which made my infertility more difficult to endure.

Brandon has been the light of my life. I said before, nothing is perfect. I was wrong. Brandon is. My pride and joy; he is a good young man and was a delight as a child and a teenager. Friends always had nightmare stories of raising their teens. A sign in one of our friends' houses boldly states, "Having teenagers is like being pecked to death by a chicken." We have none of those stories with Brandon. He was a pleasure and a joy. He still is.

Because Brandon wasn't with us, I wanted to do something special so I wouldn't feel sad. Darryl found a Texas roadhouse and gas-station-turned-restaurant outside of Fredericksburg featuring Mother's Day brunch. A trip to Fredericksburg and a drive through Texas Hill Country it was.

We got up early on Sunday for our two-hour drive from Round Rock to the Hilltop Café, a little spot just outside Fredericksburg. An eclectic atmosphere greeted us right at the front door and through to the inside. On Sundays, a live gospel band plays on one side of the restaurant, but you can hear it on both sides. They also serve crab cake eggs Benedict. My favourite. It couldn't get better than this. Well, it could. Brandon could have been there with us. I was still a little sad and lonely but I would make the best of it.

After brunch, we headed to the Enchanted Rock State Natural Area for a hike. I am in my zone of genius when outdoors. Being outside has always given me a sense of contentment. Part of the reason why I didn't want to go back to an office job is the restriction of being indoors. I yearn to be outside. Hearing birds sing and consuming the sights around me awakens my senses. Outdoors, I feel alive. Indoors, I feel confined.

The main trail at the park goes to the top of a pink granite dome overlooking Texas Hill Country in all directions. Texas is hot. And we Canadians are not used to the heat. We were prepared though, with water, sunscreen, and hats. We commenced our hike up the massive granite dome. In no rush, we would take short breaks and sip some water. Maybe spot a roadrunner in the grass and try to catch a picture of the speedy little bugger. I can see why there is a cartoon about the funny little bird.

Darryl is not the adventurous type. I am not an extreme-adventure, mountain-climbing, bungee-jumping soul either. Safety first. But I do like to challenge myself and do new things. We were nearing the top of the dome. The rock was not steep but you needed to watch your step or you could take a nasty tumble backwards. There was a slight step up, maybe about a foot in height, impeding our gradual ascent to our destination. At the top of the step there was an angle that could be tricky to traverse if you weren't careful. We had assessed from the bottom what looked to be the best way to make your way to the top of the dome. This little impediment was not visible from our scouting location. We are planners. Planners to a fault sometimes. And sometimes Darryl and I both find it hard to bend when things don't work out as planned. This seemingly large obstacle was not in the plan. Darryl didn't like it.

Warily, I found my way over the step without wiping out. I turned around to see Darryl pacing back and forth in front of the obstacle, as if in time it just might get smaller. "I'm stuck here."

"Just step up." I said.

"No. I am stuck here." Placing his hands on his hips and pursing his lips, he continued to assess the situation, nearly ready to give up and make his way back down. Darryl wasn't one for proper hiking garb; neither am I, really. Darryl is simpler in his footwear and usually owns two pairs of shoes—one black pair and one brown pair. Now that he didn't need two pairs of shoes for work, he was down to a lone pair of brown running shoes. Shoes that were nice enough to wear with tan khakis and plain enough to go with shorts or jeans. I am certain his shoes were not sturdy enough to be hiking steep hills. As long as he stayed horizontal, he'd be fine.

When you are married to someone for twenty-three years, you know what they are thinking by their mannerisms. It's a silent communication tool those with a deep bond share. I could tell from Darryl's pursed lips and hand on hips pose that he was getting ready to give up. That's his "I have no idea how to figure this out" pose. I had to intervene before it was too late.

"Darryl," with more force this time, "come this way and just step up." My stern but gentle voice beckoned him to keep trying. Too much force and he might get ticked off. I know he gave me a dirty look from behind his sunglasses. He put his hand on the rock, carefully found his footing, and overcame his obstacle.

"See. You can do it." Chalk one up for Darryl. It may not seem impressive but when someone is dealing with a fear of heights, dread can flood your instinct with flight syndrome. He did it. This was Darryl's first step to opening up to other possibilities on our trip. I was going to the top and I wanted to make sure he didn't miss out on the view either. Marriage is support for one another when fear rears its ugly head. We all need a little push sometimes.

Note to Self: Make sure to use compassion when travelling with your spouse and don't forget to add a dose of tough love to boot.

Recounting this episode of our hike to Brandon, I learned something. The same obstacle can appear differently through the lens of another person.

While I explained the rock step as being no more than a foot high, Darryl described it as being at least a two-foot steep incline. The same obstacle was much larger in Darryl's mind, a mind with a fear of heights and what might happen if he slipped and fell. I had to coach him through what I saw as a small step; no obstacle at all.

Chapter 10

Opposites Attract

Darryl is a numbers guy. Give him a calculator and he can keep himself busy for hours. He is constantly running numbers in his head. Me? I could care less about numerical details. Start talking numbers and I start wondering why the sky is blue.

What made me first take notice of Darryl was how good he was with children. I knew he would make a good father someday and I wanted a good father for my kids. He could talk and relate to any munchkin; a beautiful quality in any man.

I have never seen Darryl yell or scream. He has the patience of Job. Perhaps that is why we make a good pair. I was high-strung and he wasn't, so we wouldn't have explosive arguments. I did not want arguments in our house. When he is annoyed with me, I get the look. I thought only women gave the so-called look but Darryl has a look. Instead of yelling at me, he cocks his head to the side, purses his lips and slightly rolls his eyes. His body gets kind of stiff so if I am not looking directly at his face, I can tell, I'm getting the look. Like when I take too long picking a bag of trail mix and he is thinking, *Pick a freaking bag already*.

Darryl's patience is his virtue. He will wait patiently for me while I take photos, shop for clothes or meander through the aisles of the grocery store. He is always with me. My constant rock.

I, on the other hand, have very little patience. I can be bossy and when I ask for something to be done, I want it done now. Darryl consistently says he will get to it later. It's funny because I always said I would never marry a man that watched sports, and that I would marry a man who was mechanically inclined. Darryl watches any and all sports, even darts. He's fanatical about football. Mechanical issues? I'm the one that wields the hammer. Darryl is no Mr. Fix-it.

Darryl loves to drive for great distances without stopping. I can hardly keep my eyes open if I'm in a car for half an hour. Whenever he wants me to wake up, he makes the most annoying, loud, over-exaggerated yawning sound with a gurgle at the end. Two of those yawns and my seat is back in the upright position.

I eat almost anything and I adore seafood. Darryl does not. Most of our disagreements come from choosing where to eat out. For Darryl, Heaven's banquet will be prepared with peanut butter, bread, eggs, and hamburgers. I like all those things too, just not every day.

Call me Sherlock as I will dive into any mystery to figure out the plot. Darryl's favourite saying used to be, "If I was the peanut butter, where would I be?" As he would open the cupboard and expect to find whatever he was looking for right in front of him.

"Right here," I would say, walking by him and opening an entirely different cupboard and handing him the peanut butter jar.

Darryl is a pretty quiet guy. He's laid back and likes to watch the situation unfold. When a situation gets out of hand, though, he tends to freeze up. Travelling doesn't always mean leaving the country. When we first moved to Sylvan Lake from Saskatchewan, we decided we would spend time exploring our immediate area. One day, Darryl, Brandon and I went to Bower Ponds in Red Deer.

The day of infamy came with perfect weather. The skies were blue, the sun was shining, families were running in the park. People take advantage of nice days in the summer in Canada since the season is so short. Bower Ponds was packed. It's a pretty area.

There is a large pond in the centre of the park that is big enough for people to kayak and paddleboat. The grass covered hills stretch up the sides of the pond like a natural outdoor amphitheater. People dotted the hills with their multi-coloured picnic blankets and water toys. We decided to rent a paddleboat.

Brandon was five years old at the time so he sat in the middle. Darryl got in first and took the right side of the boat. I got in last and took the left side. Off we paddled, happily watching the ducks in the water as the tendrils of our wake drifted behind us. A lovely, perfect family outing.

Darryl is tall. He's 6'4" and his legs were getting cramped up. He also does not know how to swim.

We paddled back to the dock and the attendant put out a hook to pull us in. She made a fatal error, though, as she pulled us straight in rather than lining up Darryl's side with the dock. Gingerly and with wobbly legs, Darryl tried to stand up but the bow of the boat started to sink. Darryl quickly sat down. *Okay, now what?* Darryl stood up again. And again, the bow started to sink. This isn't good. *Three times a charm?* For the third time, Darryl stood up and like the Titanic, our sad little boat sunk. I grabbed Brandon and threw him to the deck before we capsized. Down I went into the icy depths of Bower Ponds. But note, it is called Bower "Ponds." The water isn't deep. I stood up to see Darryl stretched out perpendicular over the water. His hands like eagle's talons bored into the wood of the dock. His feet were like a fisherman's anchor, clasped to the now emerged boat.

"Darryl. Let go and stand up," I yelled.

"I can't. I'll sink."

"Darryl. Let go and stand up." I said slower and with more potency this time. "Look. It's not deep."

His body was beginning to shake from the stress, as linking himself between the land and boat was taking its toll. He stared down at the water as if it would be his final demise. Within seconds that seemed to span hours, Darryl let go and went down into the water.

We gave the spectators at Bower Ponds a good show that day. It took us about an hour to dry off before heading home. We had embarrassed ourselves and our son. On the bright side, I know we made at least one person laugh in the park.

Looking back on this tale from our past I can see how much Darryl and I have changed since we baptized ourselves in Bower Ponds. We used to live the typical family life; a mortgage, a child and two jobs. A young family trying to find its way in the world; its parents trying to build a happy life by climbing the corporate success ladder. If you would have told me both Darryl and I would be "jobless" and "homeless" in just over a decade, I would have laughed in your face. No way would that happen. We had life planned. But plans don't always work out the way we anticipate, do they?

Part 2 – Chrysalis

Chapter 11

Egypt

After one month work-travelling in Texas, it was time to go back to Calgary for my convocation from SAIT. Darryl and I flew back to Calgary and met up with Brandon, who had taken some time off work to attend my graduation ceremony. If you think it would feel weird to have your twenty-year old son see you cross the stage to obtain your college diploma, you are right. It's funny, but even now that I'm a grown-up, I want approval from people I love. When I was a child, I had a strong desire to be liked. I wanted to be the popular one. The one who was at the top of the class. The one that everyone wanted to be with. I was an overachiever and wanted to be perfect. I wanted to be the best at everything I did and I didn't like to make mistakes. I wanted my parents to be proud of me. Now, I hoped Darryl and Brandon were proud of me for what I had accomplished.

Our program was the last class to cross the stage to receive our diplomas. It was otherworldly waiting behind the scenes, everyone standing in a single row, nerves of excitement electric in the atmosphere. "Is my hat straight?" "How's my hair?" Everyone lent a helping hand to make sure everyone looked their best in their moment in the spotlight. And then, you are up next and your name is called. I know I was beaming, just like the rest of my classmates as they walked up and accepted their right into the SAIT alumni. As I stood and accepted my diploma, a deep-booming voice yelled out from the back of the auditorium, "That's my mom." My smile grew a mile. Brandon was proud of me. Those three words meant more to me than the piece of paper I now held in my hand. There I was, in my black convocation gown and cap, a gold stole and medallion from my sorority around my neck. I had earned those colours for my 4.0 GPA. My one faux pas? My trusty (and dusty) travel sandals poking out from below my crisp black graduation gown. One of our instructors had commanded, "Wear nice shoes," when prepping us for grad. *Sorry, I just landed from Texas and I'm headed to Egypt.* The only other shoes I owned were grey running shoes with neon orange laces, perfect for travel miles but even worse for fancy occasions than sandals. *I have become a travel bum*, I thought. And I couldn't have been happier about it.

That very night we had flights booked for Cairo, Egypt. Why not top off graduation with a bang? Our itinerary would start in Egypt and take us to Jordan. We would then fly to Italy, pick up our leased car and drive up through Europe. Darryl and I are consummate planners, but this time, we didn't have a lot planned. We wanted to go with the flow, for the first time in our lives, and not have everything booked ahead of time. It was alarming but intoxicating at the same time. We felt like teenagers that had snuck out with our parents' car and nothing but a case of beer in the trunk.

Seventeen hours later and we were no longer in Calgary; we were standing and staring dumbfounded at a massive crowd of people outside the Cairo airport. Stunned by the commotion around us, our only prayer was to find our driver. He had to be somewhere in the multitude of faces.

We wanted to have our own guide so that we understood the attractions we were visiting and their historical significance. We had, in some countries, encountered the local panhandlers following us around trying to sell us needless souvenirs. Our guide would protect us from this unwanted solicitation.

Our driver spotted us, standing there totally daft. We didn't need to worry about finding him; he found us and I'm sure we were easy to pick out. The only two people standing there with our mouths open, eyes fixated on the horde in disbelief.

"Charlotte?" A smiling man with curly brown hair asked.

"Ibrahim?" I waited for his reply before offering any other information.

"Yes. Yes. Come with me." He took my bag and we followed him into the Egyptian night and away from the throngs of people. I couldn't believe it. We were in Egypt. We made our way to Ibrahim's car, which of course, was blocked in by other cars.

"Welcome to Cairo," said Ibrahim with a huge, beaming smile. Ibrahim had a pleasant demeanour and was excited to see us. Instantly, we felt comfortable with him. He was well dressed in casual street clothes. His friendly, trustworthy eyes were the friend that what we needed in that moment. It was after 2:00 a.m. We were hot and tired, like two wilting leaves drooping on a branch. *Just please get us to our hotel so we can acclimate to our new surroundings and get some sleep,* I was silently praying as we stood on the smoldering pavement in the dark of the Cairo night. There was a business phone number on the car. Ibrahim called the number and eventually someone came and moved the car so we could get out. We piled into the small automobile, suitcases in the trunk, and headed away from the airport to our next destination, which I dearly hoped would be our hotel.

As he drove, Ibrahim's car would make a funny grinding noise as it went over bumps. He stopped the vehicle, shook his head, got out and banged on the rear driver's side wheel well. Whatever was loose was hammered back into place because the grinding stopped. On we went through the bustling streets of Cairo in the wee hours of the morning. Families whizzed by us on motorbikes, often with dad driving and mom holding onto three children, all of whom were not wearing helmets. It was astounding to me how many young children were on the streets so late at night, or early in the morning.

"It's the end of Ramadan," Ibrahim said. "Everyone is out celebrating." *Ah, okay. That makes sense.*

We drove, and we drove, and we drove. What seemed like an eternity was getting close to an hour. *Would this night-time, live movie scene ever end?* By this point, I was starting to get a little freaked out. *Where in the world was Ibrahim taking us? Where is our hotel? Had we just been swindled by a possible rip-off artist targeting unknowing tourists?* The direction our car was going was cause for concern. We drove under bridges, on dirt roads beside canals piled high with garbage. Not to mention the stench of sewer. *He is going to take us somewhere, rob us and kick us out; or worse, kill us and throw us in the garbage.* My mind fired up by telling me horror stories. Maybe Ibrahim wasn't so trustworthy after all.

The car lurched quickly around a corner and there they were. The gates to the front of our hotel. They were almost as beautiful as the Gates of Heaven. I was grateful to finally be there. Ibrahim spoke with the guards and drove us up to the front doors. The hotel looked decent, but I couldn't say the same for the surrounding area. The dirt roads were full of garbage. Any shops that we did drive by looked less than appealing to visit. Men sitting outside smoking hookah pipes were the only signs of human life near the hotel. I imagine they were out so late at night because of Ramadan celebrations. Right across from the hotel was a large bridge that looked like it might have a troll from *Three Billy Goats Gruff* sitting underneath it, and tourists were his favourite meal. There were no trees, no grass. It was barren. "Please, please, do not go outside on the streets by yourself," warned Hassan, the man who ran the tour company we booked with. *Don't worry, Hassan, we aren't going anywhere.*

Ibrahim carried our bags inside and took off. Darryl and I proceeded to the check-in desk. Two weary, sweaty, dazed travellers, just ready to get inside our room and crash. A few hours in Egypt and we were already experiencing full-blown culture shock. *What had we gotten ourselves into?* We drove for an hour from the airport to arrive who knows where. We were getting over the shock (and relief) that Ibrahim wasn't going to murder us. I was shattered that there was nowhere to go outside the hotel. I love exploring the streets but now we were trapped in our hotel for the next couple of days. I had hoped to go outside and do some shopping on our own. You know, stroll the streets like we were in the Milan shopping district. There were no restaurants to check out. No coffee shops to get a cup of Joe. I was exhausted and disappointed at my first impression of Egypt.

"Passports please." The man behind the front desk did not look happy. Smiling was not in his repertoire. At this time of morning, it wasn't in ours either. He was dressed in a suit, roasting in the heat of the lobby.

We handed over our Canadian passports, which is required everywhere you go in Egypt.

"There is a problem. Your booking says you are Americans. These are Canadian passports."

"Yes, we are Canadians. We are not Americans." *Oh, dear Lord, please let us in our rooms. What will we do now?* I tried to message Hassan but of course he was sleeping.

"Fine. We will accept this for now. You can go to your room. We will address this in the morning." *Thank you sweet Jesus. Get me into air conditioning and a clean bed.* Thankfully, the room was decent and the air conditioner worked great. It was time to sleep and dream of the sights in Egypt we would see. Sights I had always fantasized of seeing but never believed it would happen.

We spent the next day adjusting from jet lag and absorbing where we were on the planet. First things first, breakfast. We made sure to get up in time for breakfast because it was included with our room. There was nowhere else to eat so if we missed it; we had no options. I stepped out onto our balcony. It was good to see Egypt in the daytime and in a new light. Across from the hotel were what appeared to be residential apartments. Most of the units didn't have glass in the windows so I don't know if they were vacant or if Egyptians just didn't want windows. Some balconies had shabby blankets and pieces of clothing hanging on clothes lines. There was a lot of traffic. All the vehicles were small vans, cars or trucks. They looked old and run down. Right beside the hotel was a lot that was nothing but dirt and smashed up pieces of concrete. There was a small, square shack of stone near the front of the lot that had people living in it. The area around us was not much different in the light. It was a dump.

Our room overlooked the pool area. Thankfully, this part was a tiny oasis in a valley of despair. The large, kidney shaped pool was clean. There were tables, reclining chairs and umbrellas on the deck. No one was swimming yet. It was breakfast. Time to eat.

Breakfast was buffet style and the food was good. There were pastries, meats and fruit. The service style in Egypt is quite different than in Canada. People were not eager to help and they didn't smile. We had to approach the staff if we wanted to ask any questions. No one came over to our table to offer any assistance. They all stood at a distance and watched the people eat.

It was time to contact Hassan to straighten out our passport issue. "Oh, we just call you Americans. It is the same thing." He stated matter-of-factly. *Um. No. It's not.* The United States of America is a different country than Canada. It would be like us calling Egyptians Sudanese because Sudan is south of the country and you are from the same continent. We have different views, different histories. Just like the different African countries do. I hoped there would be no further issues with this as he had booked all our accommodations and travel for this trip. *Don't worry about that now… It's time to see the pyramids.*

Off we were, back in the car to see the ultimate bucket-list attraction.

"Look. Look." I leaned over and poked Darryl in the side. "There they are." Right in front of us, outside the car window, were the massive pyramids of stone, built thousands of years ago. I couldn't wait to touch them and stand on them. The only remaining structures of the original Seven Wonders of the Ancient World and we are about to experience them in the flesh. *Just. Breathe.*

The ancient sites in Egypt are beyond imagination. All my life I had dreamed of this moment and now it was here, but it still felt like a dream. The haziness of the air over Giza increased the dream feeling. Walking up to the pyramids and surveying the area was like being in a mirage. Except it wasn't a mirage. It was real and Darryl and I were experiencing this dream together. I'd tell Darryl to pinch me but that might give him other ideas.

Darryl is a city boy and I am a farm girl. He really had no interactions with animals until he met me, so he isn't very comfortable around livestock. It took me a decade to get him to agree to a horse-driven carriage ride in Banff.

When you arrive at the pyramids, you are free to explore the three main pyramids on your own. Then you have the option to take either a horse-driven carriage or a camel ride to see the Great Sphynx of Giza. I wanted the camel ride, but I knew this would be a long shot.

"Do you want to take the camels or the carriage?" This was a no brainer, but I thought I'd try.

"Carriage," was Darryl's short reply. No questions, no hesitation. There was no way he was climbing up on the back of a camel and riding down to the Sphinx. It wouldn't have mattered what kind of animal it was. Darryl does not ride animals. Horse, cow, donkey—if it has fur and four legs, he won't ride it. Just the thought of it makes him screw up his face like someone who just smelled a skunk.

"Oh. But first, you must get on the camel for a picture." Our guide was very enthusiastic about getting us on a camel. I was game. I was in a skirt so it would be awkward, but hey, I'm in Egypt and I need my camel photo op. I went first, knowing Darryl was dreading what was coming next. His turn.

Yes, Darryl's turn. Darryl can say no to me but apparently, he can't say no to a persuasive tour guide. Gingerly, and with the face of a terrified child, Darryl threw one leg over the camel's saddle. With a shove off his left leg, he was fully situated on the beast. I had my camera phone ready. This was an epic moment that I knew I would never witness again. The guide and I gave instructions to Darryl on how to hold on and steady his balance with the camel. In my mind, I could see Darryl toppling ass over tea kettle and ending up face first in the sands of the Sahara. Darryl is a big guy and when he falls, he falls hard.

Before the camel's ascent, Darryl listened to the guide like someone preparing for a final exam. Surely, if he missed anything, disaster would occur. The camel began to rise. It got up on its front knees. Darryl's facial expression shifted from one of intense focus to one of intense fear. Every muscle in his body clenched. His mouth was clasped shut. Then the camel's back end started to rise. Darryl's bottom lip sucked into his mouth and his teeth clenched down on his lip as hard as his hands clamped onto the saddle horn.

"Lean back. Lean back," the guide and I both yelled at Darryl. He had to lean against the camel's back or he would certainly fall off. In slow motion, the camel lifted his front right leg and started to level off. Darryl started to smile. At the change in his attitude from terror to sheer joy, the guide and I burst out laughing. The camel was up on all fours now and Darryl's smile was as wide as the ocean. His hand shot up into the air, fingers spread wide open like he had just won a world championship. Darryl had conquered the world. I had never seen him like that before. It was a brilliant moment of transformation.

We had a few different guides, all of them were Egyptologists. Their knowledge of the attractions is priceless when you visit. From explaining the hieroglyphics to how the structures were built and the culture stemming from the ancients, it is far more than you read about in books. Walking through the sites humbles you as a person. It is at these moments you realize how big the world is and how you are a small part in the grand scheme of things. This is truly an incredible world we live in.

Where else can we experience the history and different cultures on such a raw level as we can within the actual country itself? The culture of Egypt is radically different than the culture of Canada. We walk freely on the streets in Canada. We wear whatever we want—some people need to seriously look in a mirror before they step outside—but we are allowed the freedom to make choices. This is not the case in Egypt. We did not walk the streets alone. The "human mosquitoes" would be all over us. Note, this is a term given by the Egyptians to the peddlers on the streets who sell inadequate souvenirs to unknowing tourists. We were warned not to buy the papyrus scrolls that were wrapped in plastic as they are cheap imitations made from a leaf that is toxic to humans.

The garbage everywhere was overwhelming. I was surprised that the streets didn't reek like rotten corpses in the heat. Most of the garbage seemed to be paper and plastics. I guess that is why there was no smell. It looked like someone took a massive garbage can and dumped the contents every 6 metres. We watched at the train station as one young boy, around the age of twelve, took a bottle of water he no longer wanted, dumped out the remaining contents, and threw the bottle on the ground. There was no sense of pride on keeping the streets clean. *What has caused this carelessness? How do you re-instill the common sense to throw your garbage into the can made for the purpose of keeping the streets clean?*

In Luxor, we saw a freshly gutted and skinned cow lying on the street. Just lying there, innards gleaming and exposed to the sweltering sun. *Was this lunch?* As passengers in the back seat of the car, Darryl and I looked at each other. *Did we just see that? Was it real?* We drove by again awhile later and all that remained of the carcass was the head and a blood trail, mingled with the dirt from the street, leading into an old building.

Note to Self: Don't order the beef at lunch.

Living in a country where English is the first language most people learn holds privileges we take for granted. It is also a crutch—I wish I had paid closer attention in French class so many years ago. We are fortunate so many countries learn English. We would be even more fortunate if we took the time to learn and master more than two or three languages. The doors of communication would be blown wide open. Do we hold a snobbish attitude of the English language, expecting everyone to be able to understand us and to speak our language as well?

As a woman in Canada, we also take our freedom of choice for granted. I knew Egypt was a predominantly Muslim country. I took a scarf along with me in case I would need to cover my shoulders at certain attractions. We were in Egypt in June. Being Canadian, we are used to cooler weather. Hot is 25 degrees Celsius. It was 40 degrees Celsius every day we were in Egypt. I had sleeveless shirts and nobody was going to tell me I couldn't wear them. Nobody did. At least I don't think they did. Women got into the swimming pools dressed in their full burkas. I didn't go for a swim because I was too uncomfortable putting on a swimsuit with fully clothed women in the pool. Now here I was, feeling totally exposed on a train platform.

We were standing on the platform at the Giza train station. I was wearing a red, sleeveless cotton shirt. It had a high neck so no cleavage was showing. I was also wearing a floor length skirt. The train station was filthy—surprise, surprise. Garbage was piled up outside the train station entrance. Empty bottles and papers littered the train tracks. The platform was packed with people waiting for their trains. Darryl and I were booked on a sleeper train from Giza to Aswan where we would then get on a three-night Nile River cruise. I had the picture of a lovely, cozy train with two little beds and a dining car where we would eat our meals. It was a fantasy. A fantasy that turned into a nightmare.

Ibrahim was our driver again this day and he stayed on the platform with us until our train arrived, *God bless his soul*. Trains were announced but there was no English anywhere. No English announcements, no English signs. We had our tickets with the train number on them but there were no numbers on the trains either. *How in the world would anyone on their own who didn't speak the native tongue know what train to get on?*

Train after train pulled into the station. *"Dear God, please don't let this be our train,"* was all I could think each time a train pulled up. The trains looked like they had been to hell and back. Dark, dirty and dingy with masses of people hanging out the doors. The stench of urine would permeate the platform with each passing train. Ibrahim would look at us and say, "That's not your train."

There was a family sitting on the ground that included what looked like a mother, grandmother, father, three young girls ranging around eight to twelve years old, and a little boy about two years of age. The little boy was acting up something fierce. He was slapping his mother in the face and kicking her. She did nothing to stop him and neither did anyone else. There was absolutely no discipline for the child. *Give me two days with that kid,* I thought. The girls were looking at me. Being the only blonde woman on the platform drew attention, along with my sleeveless shirt. After staring at me for a while, the kids came up to me saying things in a nasty tone. Their body language didn't offer any aspect of friendship either. I had no idea what they were saying to me, and frankly, I didn't care. I was melting and just wanted my train to show up so I could get out of there. "We can move to another spot," Ibrahim said, sensing my discomfort.

"No. That's fine," I said. *Where else could we go?* The platform was packed with people and nobody looked like I did. Now I knew what it felt like to be a minority. How sheltered a life I had lived in Canada. Our former travel choices were ones promising a sense of comfort and familiarity. I realized how I missed the comforts of home. Sweat poured down my legs. Chafing on my inner thighs burned from the salty perspiration. My wants were reduced to needs. I needed my train and I needed air conditioning.

Finally, our train arrived—forty-five minutes late. The train was not terrible, but it was not great either. Our room did have air conditioning—my prayers were answered. Darryl and I both sat and took a few breaths to unwind. The Giza train station was the only time we felt uncomfortable in Egypt. The experience was quite unnerving so to be in our little room was a welcome relief. We shut the door and closed off the world.

Reality has a funny way of returning, though. The room was tiny. There were two seats and our beds were folded into the wall. There was a small cupboard with a sink the size of a small soap dish sunken in the middle of the vanity. There was a tiny tap for water for handwashing only. Two tiny bags of liquid soap were next to the sink. The doors on the vanity wouldn't stay shut and they clanged open with every turn of the train. I jostled my suitcase up against them to keep them shut. There was hardly room for our two suitcases and our feet on the floor. After sweating buckets all day, I just wanted to have a shower and get into my jammies. My inner thighs still burned like fire. There would be no shower. The bathroom was down the hall and you really didn't want to go in there without a hazmat suit on. A tiny metal toilet with the hole opening to the tracks below was to be our throne. At least there was a small sink in the bathroom to wash our hands.

Note to Self: Wet wipes are life-savers and showers are not as internationally available as you'd hope.

The conductor came around and explained how the meals would work, when he would turn down our beds, and when he would wake us up in the morning for our arrival at Aswan. The meals were meager, but enough. There was a small, hot dish served in a foil container. It was a chicken casserole with potatoes, lightly seasoned with cumin, garlic and paprika. There was a slice of bread and a honey cake for dessert. It was like a sponge cake and about the size of a tootsie roll. An Egyptian TV dinner of sorts, minus the TV.

The sleeper car beds were uncomfortable and I slept like crap. One would think the rocking and rolling of the train would put you to sleep. Not a chance. Someone was smoking in a nearby room and it choked me throughout the night. *Couldn't they put out that damn cigarette?* I guess the Giza train station had stressed them out as much as it had us.

About three times during the night, the train horn went off, after which there was a sudden thud. *What in the world did we just hit?* The train would never slow down and often it felt as if we were on a roller coaster headed around the bend. I envisioned the train going off the rails. Once again, thoughts of death danced into my subconscious. Then the fear of bed bugs found its way in there too. Immediately, I began to itch. There was no way I was getting a decent sleep. I never considered myself a demanding person until now. I wanted comfort, and I wanted it pronto.

Darryl was on the bed underneath my bunk. He was silent all night. We both were. I didn't dare say anything just in case he was truly sleeping. Although, I should have realized he wasn't because there was no snoring from the depths below.

Our train arrived at Aswan around 8:00 a.m. Darryl and I showered with the wet naps that I brought along. At least I was prepared for hygiene shortages. Even though we did not have a restful sleep, the previous day was over and we put it behind us. We were ready to meet our new guide that would accompany us for the next three days as we sailed up the Nile River back to Luxor, enjoying the incredible sights of Egypt along the way.

There is no better way than travel to move from the known to the unknown. Challenging ourselves to interact with the unfamiliar was the best way for Darryl and me to expand our intelligence. All five of our senses came to life, the key to doing this was to get over our stumbling blocks of fear and push ourselves to try new experiences. Sight, taste, touch, smell, hearing—travel highlights them all, and I can think of no other place where my five senses were heightened more than in Egypt. Magical historic sites such as the Valley of the Kings, authentic foods like fresh sugar cane juice, textiles such as real papyrus scrolls, odours of sweat mingled with camel hair in the blistering heat of midday, and let us not forget the sounds of the train horn belting out into the night to warn someone or something of their impending demise. Our previous anxieties had held us back from visiting these places we perceived to be different or possibly even dangerous. Letting go of these anxieties helped us to take the leap and explore the world around us.

Egypt challenged me in ways I never thought possible. It also revealed personality traits I didn't realize I had. I never considered myself high maintenance, *but was I?* There were things I took for granted in my life that I now missed. Clean streets. The ability to walk by myself wherever I wanted with no hesitation. Traffic rules. Cars where all four doors stay closed while the vehicle was in motion. Air-conditioned buildings. Wi-Fi—glorious Wi-Fi—everywhere. Free, drinkable water from the tap. Unwinding the day with a glass of wine. And real coffee from ground beans. I was dying for a cup of good coffee. If there are two indulgences in my life I favour the most, they are coffee and wine. I have been known to say if I had to give up one or the other, coffee would be the one thing I cannot live without.

I was spoiled, and Egypt showed me how spoiled I was. We have everything we can possibly want and more to a ridiculous amount of excess. Now, I saw how rich we were in the eyes of the world. I was fully aware of what I took for granted at home. It may sound like I didn't enjoy Egypt. That is not true. There were things I did not expect and was not prepared for. I experienced culture shock, and I threw myself into it wholeheartedly. That being said, ten days in Egypt was enough. I was ready to go. Jordan was calling.

Chapter 12

Jordan

Stepping onto the streets of Amman for the first time brought a feeling of absolute freedom after the ten days we had spent in Egypt. Jordan and Egypt are two very different countries. Amman was a surprisingly modern destination compared to Cairo. The streets were busy, and traffic was still crazy, but they were clean. Bright lights encircled palm trees and were strung across the streets bringing a welcoming, warm, and safe feeling to the city. Our group of nine walked the streets without harassment. For our trip to Jordan, we booked with G Adventures, a Canadian based tour company with a great reputation. I am a challenge hunter but I did not want to be on my own for my first visit to the Middle East. Our family was worried about us being in Jordan with it being so close to Syria and all the scary news originating from that country. "Jordan is safe", I assured them. "It is the safest country in the Middle East." My words of comfort were words of truth.

After visiting the ancient city of Jerash, our group stopped for a buffet lunch. The restaurant was clean and inviting with a man baking fresh flatbreads outside in a stone oven. We all sat in a group on the deck with a lovely view of the city. This was the perfect place to use the bathroom since the surroundings were immaculate. I excused myself from the table and went to use the facilities.

Throughout our travels, I had a handy-dandy waterproof fanny pack. To my delight, fanny packs were coming back into style after decades of being shunned. I don't care how they look, they are convenient for travel. I hung my pack up on the hook on the door and proceeded to do my business. *Brief interlude here…*

Okay, now, how do I flush this thing? There was no chain with a handle hanging from the ceiling. There were no levers on the side of the toilet; however, there was a paddle beside the latrine on the floor. *Hmm, I guess I push that with my foot.*

Note to Self: Never push a lever on a toilet
unless you are certain of what it will do.

As soon as I pushed the paddle down, a clean, cold, heavy duty stream of water shot out all over my abdomen. I jumped to the side to escape the deluge and the water shot all over my fanny pack. It would not stop. The door was soaked. The floor was soaked. Hands flailing, I stepped on the paddle again to release it. Talk about putting on the brakes. Finally, the spouting water subsided. But, there I stood, the front of me soaking wet. *This is going to look great.* I strapped my fanny pack back on and headed back to our table. Thankfully, I was wearing black capris that day and a multi-coloured shirt. No one at the table noticed I had nearly been drowned by a toilet. Smiling, I sat down and proceeded to eat my scrumptious lunch, wet and uncomfortable, but good food cures anything.

Jordan is a country steeped in history. I had taken a module in school about Jordan and as soon as I completed it, I knew I had to go. The historical biblical sites of great significance such as Mount Nebo and Bethany Beyond the Jordan where Jesus was baptized are in Jordan. Standing on the top of Mount Nebo and looking at the Promised Land from where Moses last stood and died carried with it a deep, spiritual feeling. The greatest prophet recognized in all religions and who wrote the first five books of the *Bible* stood here and saw the same sights I was looking at today.

The view from the top of Mount Nebo is vast. The hills are brown and stretch from the left to the right. There is an occasional tree and small scattered bushes. A haze covered the horizon from the heat of the day and the sandy soil. From this point, on a clear day, our guide told us we could see Jerusalem. Alas, we could not see the Holy City. The sky was clear and appeared as blue as the ocean hovering over the haze. God promised Moses a land flowing with milk and honey and from this point, there is only desert hills. I wondered if, after wandering in the desert for forty years, Moses wondered like I did where the milk and honey were. To me, a land of promise is covered with green grass, tall palm trees, rivers, and wildlife—an oasis in the desert. This Promised Land was not what I envisioned, but then again, we don't see things the same way that God does. *What was the promised land that God had in store for Darryl and I?* Our promised land where I stood at the precipice obviously did not come without further obstacles. *What obstacles were coming our way and how would God lead us through them? Were we headed for a desert or an oasis?*

There is a picture of Darryl and me standing where Moses stood as he looked out on the land that his people were promised. We aren't smiling. In every other picture, we are smiling or laughing but in this picture, we look somber. Darryl in particular looks in deep thought. His brow is furrowed and he is not wearing his hat. Moses was not allowed to enter the Promised Land, he was only allowed to see what he had been searching for all those years. Darryl said Mount Nebo held the deepest spiritual experience for him. To stand where a man with such historical significance stood; seeing his dream and knowing he wouldn't enter this land, brought him to pause and ponder, *what does God have in store for us?*

There is something about exploring your religious roots and walking on the same soil—soil with such historical significance—that changes a person forever. I read about these places but seeing them has made them real. Mysteries have become clearer and stories read in the *Bible* are now easier to understand with a clarity I did not have before.

The deepest religious experience for me was our visit to Bethany Beyond the Jordan. The Jordan River is almost dried up now; it is a small creek separating Israel from Jordan. There is no water left at the historical site of Jesus' baptism. Our tour took us to what is left of the Jordan River where we could sit, dip our feet in the cool water, and watch believers on the Israel side getting baptized, setting their hearts aside for God. I felt calm and peace enter me as I watched the people in their white cotton gowns being dipped one-by-one into the waters of the Jordan. I could have sat there for hours. A silent prayer of gratitude wove through my thoughts.

Thank you, God, for bringing me to this place. For giving me the time to experience this country, right now, right here in my life. When I close my eyes, it is just me and You here, in this Holy place. I can feel Your presence, Your peace, and it fills my heart and soul with song. What a privilege to be here with my feet in the cool waters of the Jordan, washing away my burdens and refreshing my spirit.

****

"Friends, be careful and don't push yourselves today. It is hot outside," stated Zuhair, our trusted guide. It was the day to visit Petra, the Rose City. Another bucket list item I had longed to see and experience. Zuhair was right, it was hot. June is the hottest month of the year to visit Jordan. Originally, we had planned to visit Jordan in September but our desired tour was sold out. The morning walk down the Siq was cool and comfortable but by midday it was supposed to be 40 degrees Celsius outside. We were up and had breakfast by 5:30 a.m. so we could beat the crowds of tourists. An excellent plan. When we arrived at the Treasury, we were the only ones there, aside from a few local Bedouin selling camel and donkey rides. The Bedouin are an interesting group of characters. They look like Captain Jack Sparrow. So much so that one wonders if they have rum tucked into their saddle bags.

Note to Self: Next time, visit Jordan in
September when it's not as hot as a fiery furnace.

Petra is massive. The park covers 2,640 acres, which is four times the size of Manhattan. I had no idea how large the site was. I thought Petra was just the Treasury, the most iconic carved building in the Rose City. It is much more. The site is covered with carved buildings and tombs from a city thriving in trade thousands of years ago. Darryl and I walked over 16 kilometres that day. There are numerous hikes to take so we decided on the hike up to the Monastery, another rock-carved building approximately 6 kilometres from the Treasury. Eight hundred and fifty stone steps take you to the summit. The heat was oppressive, burning down on us like dry waves of fire.

The walk up to the Monastery was not too difficult for an able-bodied person. The issue arose when we decided to descend and ran out of water. Oh yeah, did I mention how hot it was that day? I have never sweat so much in my life. A good thing I suppose, as I've heard sweating means you aren't dehydrated, but I thought I was going to die. By midday, there was no escape from the grueling sun. There were no trees for shade and the cliffs only provide a sliver of relief. I made Darryl stop a few times so I could rest.

Leaning on a rock with my hands on my knees, I bowed my head and took deep breaths of air. I threw my head back and wailed to Darryl, "Where is the fucking guy selling water?" That was it. I had lost it. Here I was on the top of Mount Nebo one day and dropping an F-bomb the next. I don't like to swear but the fiery incinerator of heat and the devil whispering in my ear got to me that day.

"We have a way to go yet," Darryl said to me calmly. That was not what I wanted to hear.

"Ugh," was all I could muster. We trudged onward. This was my struggle in the desert. When would I get to my promised land flowing with cold water? *Darryl may have to carry me out. I'm not going to make it.* Darryl was thinking the same thing. I was nearing hallucinations when finally, the man who sold water close to the entrance came into view. I knew it wasn't a mirage. Water is the milk of life. And boy, that cold water was good. Darryl wouldn't have the burden of carrying me out after all.

Was it worth it? I had seen and experienced one of the most iconic historical sites on earth. I had trekked up the 850 steps to the Monastery. I had sat in the very caves where Nabateans traded with caravans thousands of years ago. I had seen ancient Roman roads and amphitheaters that I didn't know existed. I bought real myrrh oil and real frankincense resin to take home. I lived history. You bet it was worth it and I'd do it again in a heartbeat. But next time, I'll take more water.

Visiting the Middle East was a way to break out of my comfort zone. I had never been to this area of the world but had always dreamed of visiting the Holy Land. *Why couldn't Darryl and I make the dreams of our future a reality?* Fear had been holding us back. Fear and lack of confidence prevented us from making changes in our lives that would lead to the materialization of our creative visions. If we had listened to those who said there was no way they would go to Jordan during these turbulent times, we would never have had these experiences. Our dreams would still be just dreams. My dream of floating in the Dead Sea was about to come true.

There was a van that drove the hotel guests to and from the Dead Sea. It was a short, two-minute drive but the ground was not great for walking on and as usual, the sun was scorching hot. I was in my bathing suit and Darryl was in his shorts and a t-shirt. After all, he doesn't swim and had no desire to step foot into the waters. That was fine, he could watch over my belongings and take pictures.

Our part of the beach was as rocky as a gravel pit so there was no way my shoes were coming off. There was a mud pit nearby that was enclosed in a concrete circular shape like a large outdoor well. The idea was that you had to roll around in the mud and bake in the sun before entering the Dead Sea in order to get the full benefit of the healing properties. I hadn't played in the mud since I was a little girl and I admit, the idea didn't thrill me. But like a good girl, I followed directions.

I stepped into the morass and felt the mud squish between my toes. It was hot from the heat of the sun and it smelled like sewage. *I have to roll around in this goop?* Reluctantly, I sat down and proceeded to rub the mud all over my body, including my face. There was a mirror placed beside the mud pit so you could make sure you didn't miss a spot. When I was completely covered, I got up and stepped out of the pit. I felt like a swamp creature climbing out of the sewer drain.

"Okay, Darryl, time me for ten minutes. That's all the time I need to bake." Darryl was quite entertained by watching me writhe around in the cesspool. Now he got to sit in a lounge chair and watch me cook to well done. The sun started to work its magic and prepare me like a clay pot. The mud tightened up on my skin. I hated it. I don't like being dirty and can hardly stand it if there is dirt on my hands. I stood there with hands slightly outstretched because I didn't want to touch myself.

"Time's up," Darryl said enthusiastically.

When walking into the Dead Sea, it is advised to go backwards and let the water lift you up on its own. It was not easy walking backward on a rocky beach with feet soaked in mud and stuck in sandals that were not meant for this type of foray. I nearly fell over a few times but soon enough, I was up to my thighs in the water, was lifted up and swept off my feet. I bobbed in the water, legs and arms outstretched, and let the water cleanse my crusty body. The salty water splashing on my face stung. The water on my lips had a viscous consistency. It was so salty that it didn't even taste salty, it tasted like gasoline. I tried to spit the oily, vile water out but it lingered. I floated until I was free of my muddy exterior and perfectly brined. Once back on land and dried off, my skin felt soft and supple. The next day, my skin was glowing. I had a free spa day at the Dead Sea. Even though I looked like a nightmare when I backed into the Dead Sea, I emerged as a new woman, awoken from a restful sleep. Now I was prepared to tackle Italy.

Chapter 13

The Missed Panini

Speaking of nightmares, have you ever driven in Italy? Upon leaving the incredible country of Jordan, we flew to Rome to pick up the car we leased for the remainder of our journey. No more tour guides. No more groups. It was just Darryl and I. Alone. Together. 24/7. If you want to test a relationship, go travelling together. Better yet, lease a car and drive in Italy.

Italy is an in-your-face type of destination. People are everywhere and it is fast paced, particularly in the big, touristy cities like Rome, Venice, Florence and Milan. The people are loud and they talk fast. Don't get me wrong. I love Italy. It is one of my favourite destinations. You just need to be prepared for what it is like. Especially the traffic. There are scooters and Vespas everywhere. When you stop at a traffic light, they swarm you like bees to honey. Traffic rules do not apply. Streets are often narrow and passable by one vehicle only. I asked Darryl how he would describe driving in Italy. "Hectic. Depending on where you were. It was white knuckle driving. Maybe that's a little extreme. I'm thinking of the mountains and people passing on the corners. And then you have the Vespas..."

Roundabouts are everywhere in Italy. We don't have many of them in Canada but I can honestly say Darryl is now an expert. Together we would arrive safely at a destination by teaming up. Darryl would watch the road and I would watch the GPS. Sure, the GPS spoke English but those roundabouts are confusing when you aren't used to them.

A cheery, female robotic voice with a crisp, British accent would say, "Enter the roundabout and take the third exit."

"What's the third exit?" Darryl would ask.

"Pretty much just drive straight through," would be my response. First, second, third, fourth, fifth exit—if you miss it, go around again. A no brainer. For someone who drives in them all the time, that is. We always panic when we miss a corner in North America. Not to worry; just drive around the circle again until you figure it out. This was how we approached it by the time we reached Germany. Italy taught us patience. Italy also taught us not to panic, but it took almost a month in the country to ingrain that in our brains. As fast and hectic as Italy seems, the people take their time and enjoy life. They are just in a hurry to get to their next destination once behind the wheel, or a set of handlebars.

I had my first panic attack while driving in Rome. We had purposely stayed in Ostia outside of Rome because we had been to the Eternal City before and observed the irrational traffic. We spent the afternoon at the coast of the Tyrrhenian Sea and it was time to go back to the hotel. Darryl took the wrong turn and we ended up on a road headed straight to downtown Rome. In my mind, we were headed directly to disaster. As Darryl kept driving and getting closer, sweat rolled down my arms, and my heartbeat increased.

"Would you just take the next exit," I nearly screamed at him. "Just get us off this road." He was not turning around and I was ready to freak out. All I could picture was getting into an accident right in the centre of Rome's largest roundabout, Piazza Venezia. Four major roads meet on this insane traffic circle. There are no lanes. Just tons of cars and people trying to cross the street. It's a cluster fog if you ever saw one.

"Okay, okay," Darryl said, and off the next exit we went.

"Just pull over so we can get our bearings." I needed a few minutes to breathe and overcome my terrified thoughts. I was not being a good passenger to an already stressed-out driver.

Note to Self: Bring a valium if you plan on being a passenger in a vehicle in Italy. On second thought, bring two.

Driving in Italy was a gnawing fear Darryl had. He also had a fear of driving a standard transmission again. He certainly didn't need me to add to his frustrations. What I should have asked myself is, *Do I need to freak out about this?* Logic is the way to overcome the fears skulking in the recesses of our minds. My answer back now would be, *No. I don't need to freak out about this. So what? We are going the wrong way, just turn around when you have a chance.* I would then sit back and enjoy the scenery. After finding ourselves in uncomfortable situations while travelling, I now realize we can react to uncertainties in two ways: freak out or relax. Why choose the former when all it does is add to your anxiety?

Before leaving Rome, we should have changed the settings in our GPS to avoid toll highways. Obviously, it was too late once we drove onto one. *Oh well, what could go wrong?* The highway was fast and the lanes were dangerously narrow. At times it seemed as if the guardrail would take off one of the side mirrors.

An hour and a half later, we approached the gates to get off the toll road. Except, we couldn't figure out how to pay. Darryl put the little white card from our entrance on the highway into the machine. The total was just over €11. Sixteen Canadian dollars seemed pretty pricey for the drive. Of course, all the directions were in Italian so we couldn't figure out where to put a credit card to pay or where to insert money. Anxiety is the crippler of all intelligence. There was a little slot so Darryl opened it and put in €20 and closed the door. It popped back open with our money still inside. I guess it was a coin slot but we didn't have €11 in coins. Cars were lining up behind us. Embarrassed, Darryl shoved his credit card into a slot. I don't know what slot it was but it was not for a plastic card. It became jammed and he couldn't get it out. An angry Italian voice shouted at us through a loudspeaker. Stunned, we sat there, helpless as two little babies. A lady in the car behind us approached our vehicle on foot. Finally. Someone was going to help. We knew this because she was smiling. She said something in Italian and then miraculously, the arm went up and a long receipt spewed out of the machine.

"Ah," the lady said, throwing her hands up in the air, laughing.

"Ah," we mimicked our knight in shining armour, throwing our arms up, smiles beaming. I guess we get a free pass. On we went. Tuscany, here we come. We should have read the bottom of the ticket but we were too excited, and relieved, to get going. In fine print, it stated we had to pay the toll fee within two weeks at a given website address. Oops. We didn't read this until we got back to North America as we sorted our receipts. It's been almost a year and we didn't hear anything from our leased car company. I wonder if there is a warrant out for our arrest in Italy for an unpaid traffic infraction. Maybe, just maybe, they give foreigners a break.

Here is where the big test in our relationship came into play. Picture it. We were driving in the Apennine Mountain Range of Italy, the literal backbone of the country. The mountain views are glorious as we wind our way up and down the narrow mountain highway. Every once in a while, an Italian driver of a car or motorbike whizzes by us on hairpin turns. It had been a long time since breakfast and my stomach started to growl. There had not been any open restaurants for miles. At the top of the mountain our car approached a tiny panini restaurant. *Hey. There are umbrellas outside and people sitting underneath. It's open. And the views, the views are beyond magnificent. What a perfect place for lunch. The top of a mountain in Italy.* I turned to Darryl who was driving the car and asked, "Do you want to stop there for lunch?" Excitement at the possibility of eating a sandwich in this picture-perfect spot gave me goosebumps. It was exactly the experience I had been dreaming about.

"Not really," was the deadpan reply. *Did he just say that? He can't be serious.* Without a second glance, Darryl kept his gaze fixated on the road ahead and just kept driving. And there it went. The best view and the best panini in the world. Gone forever. And so were my goosebumps.

I was certain Darryl was going to say, "Sure," and pull over. After all, we hadn't seen anything open for hours. After lunch, everything closes in Italy. I mean everything. We are at the top of a mountain, on the journey of our lifetime and he said "no." It could be hours before we saw anything open again. I was dumbfounded. That feeling quickly turned to anger. How could he say, "Not really"? There was no way to turn around, the road was too narrow. When I get angry, I build up a brick wall and don't talk. Darryl was about to get the wrath of Charlotte by silent treatment. I was furious. I was robbed of my perfect Italian sandwich moment in the mountains. I glared at him and he ignored me. I know he could feel my icy daggers firing in his direction. You could cut the tension in the car with a knife. I turned my gaze to the side window. Looking at him was making me angrier.

On we drove in silence for another three hours. Yep, I was right, there was nothing open for three more hours of driving. And where did we stop to grab a bite to eat? What would be the only place open in Italy at mid-afternoon? That's right. McDonald's. I refused to eat anything but a dried up, sad little croissant along with a mediocre coffee.

Note to Self: If I hadn't been so choked, I would have noticed that I could add a beer to a burger combo meal for only €0.50. Might as well have a Happy Meal. That would have improved my mood.

"I am so mad at you. I refuse to order a burger," I scowled at Darryl, voice shaking. He gave me a disgusted look, like, *why in the world are you so mad,* which only ticked me off more. Communication, people. Breakdown in communication is where everything falls apart. I wanted to stop at the panini place. Darryl didn't want to stop driving.

"Next time you want to stop somewhere, just say we are stopping here for lunch; otherwise, I am going to keep on driving." When Darryl gets in a car to drive, he gets tunnel vision and the destination is the only thing he cares about. I like the journey. I want to stop and enjoy the view. *Wasn't the whole point of this trip to enjoy the views? Let's drive instead of taking the train so we can stop wherever we want?* So, we had come to a win/win decision. Next time I wanted to stop I would say so. Darryl would not argue and he would pull the car over. Case closed. Relationship saved. Twenty-three years of marriage was not going to be ended by a missed panini.

Chapter 14

Guido

Venice was our next stop and our budget was limited since we were travelling for an extended time. We chose to stay in an Airbnb in Mirano and Guido was our host. I'm glad we were on a budget because it forced us to stay in the smaller communities within a half hour's travel time to the big cities. Guido's apartment looked nice and modern. It was completely renovated and it fell in our price range. It had all the amenities we also required: a kitchen, private bathroom, washing machine, free parking and Wi-Fi. Book it, Danno.

Airbnb is an online platform used by house or apartment owners to rent out their space to visitors. When searching for an Airbnb, pay close attention to the pictures and description of the property. Take the reviews with a grain of salt. We used this platform to book apartments rather than staying in hotels because we could choose what amenities we wanted such as air conditioning, Wi-Fi, washing machines, a full kitchen and free parking. We also decided on a budget so you can narrow your search down by price. When travelling for an extended period, a kitchen and washing facilities are important. We didn't have to find laundry mats and we could shop at local grocery stores. Buying groceries in Europe is a treat. There are so many different varieties of food, wine, and beer, and the prices are super cheap compared to Canada. Eating out for every meal also gets too expensive.

It was a hot evening when we arrived at Guido's house. A charming, elderly man greeted us when we arrived. His smile was welcoming and he immediately showed us around. Guido's eyes danced with delight and mischief. He was in a hurry because he was going to be late for yoga since we had arrived a bit later in the day.

"I will now drive you by the train station and grocery store," Guido said, and hopped into his car. *How nice. He was going to show us exactly where to go.* Off we went, following Guido as he sped by the train station, slowed down, then pointed where it was and where we could park. Next, he took us around corners and pointed at the grocery store as he hurried off to catch his yoga class.

There is an emphasis on mingling with locals when you travel. Darryl and I are both outgoing introverts. Kind of sounds ridiculous. *An outgoing introvert? What is that, anyway?* We can be outgoing in certain situations and around certain people. At other times, we both like to hang back and watch the situation unfold. There are times when we want to get out and chat with people and other times when we don't want to talk at all. We aren't the nightlife type so our mingling with locals usually revolves around the people who work at restaurants or attractions, or the people we meet while sitting at the bar in a local pub. It is unlikely that we would approach someone on the street and start chatting.

Meeting locals is even more difficult if you don't speak their language. Guido, on the other hand, was very curious about us and wanted to visit. He didn't care that his English was rough and we didn't speak Italian. Guido was labelled a Super Host on Airbnb for a reason. When Guido returned from yoga (which he missed due to our tardiness) he invited us down for a glass of homemade limoncello under the oak tree in his yard. Little did we know this would be a budding relationship between people who lived on separate sides of the globe.

We visited with Guido late into the night. Even with his broken English, we managed to communicate. Our Italian was limited to "Ciao, Bella!" but we could understand the gist of what Guido was telling us. Over the course of our four-night stay at Guido's, he shared stories and pictures of his family and the house in which we were staying. The house was his childhood home and when his family left, squatters moved in and it fell into ruins. Guido bought the place back, kicked the squatters out, and began to build his vision by renovating the house into a vacation getaway experience. The evenings couldn't have been more perfect. It was quiet and peaceful on Guido's acreage. There were no cars driving by, no traffic noise. Only the stillness of the night accompanied by Guido's stories. The perfect Italian experience.

Note to Self: Homemade limoncello goes down like honey.
You won't notice the effects until you stand up.

Feeling a little groggy the next day from too much limoncello, Darryl and I headed to Venice by train. It is true what they say about Venice. Over-tourism is a problem. There were swarms of people everywhere. Armed with a map, we decided to stop for lunch to get our point of reference. We had one day in Venice so wanted to make sure and see St. Mark's Square. With intense examination of our tourist map, we figured out where we were and headed into the Venice streets.

Venice is like a maze. We turned corners as we tried to read the street names on the sides of buildings. We crossed bridges over the canals. We back tracked, turned this way and that only to end up back at our restaurant.

Note to Self: Maps of Venice are pretty much useless. Just follow the masses if you want to get to St. Mark's Square.

Now what? Are we only going to see this area of this incredibly beautiful city? Venice is busy but it is magical. The rustic beauty of the buildings on the canals and the boats floating under the bridges is as romantic as it gets.

After about an hour of wandering aimlessly, crumpled map in hand, and looking as confused as a fish out of water, we realized all we needed to do was follow the crowds. They all seemed to be going in one direction. Hopefully, it wouldn't turn into the blind leading the blind. Through pouring rain, wide streets to narrow pathways where traffic could only go one direction single file, we finally emerged onto St. Mark's Square.

It was one of those moments of awe for me. Goosebumps erupted on my body followed by chills. The square was gorgeous. I had no idea it would be so beautiful in person. Of course, there were still people everywhere and the lineups to get into St. Mark's Basilica were intimidating and hours long. The architecture and size of the square is what struck me. The square is considered one of the finest in the world. It is surrounded on three sides with arcades of domes and arches; the symmetry is impeccable.

We had to make it back to the train station so we decided to find our way through the winding streets again, hoping we would not get lost. The way back was a little more familiar and we didn't take too many wrong turns.

Back at the station, we looked at the posted schedule to find our platform and train number. The schedule said we needed to go to platform eighteen to catch the train back to Dolo. Our ticket said our train would arrive at 18:15. We found a bench and waited patiently for our train to arrive.

The time for our train arrived but the train that pulled into the platform didn't have the right town on the display. We didn't want to get on the wrong train and end up who knows where, so we continued to wait. Another train had pulled into platform twenty-one and it did have the name of the town we were supposed to go to but it was the wrong platform. *Should we get on that train?* This is why I like to travel by car. We are in control and if we get lost, we will figure it out. If you can't figure out public transit, you are stuck there. Both trains left and we continued to wait.

"Let's go ask for help. There is an office in the train station with people working at it. They should know what's going on," I said to Darryl. We were both getting quite annoyed at this point. We were tired, hot, and confused. We didn't want to miss our train.

We took our tickets to the office and a polite, pretty Italian lady asked if she could help us. Many people in Venice speak English because it is such a popular tourist destination.

"Our train has not shown up. One pulled into the station but it had a different name on the train." I handed her our tickets. She took them and us over to an automated ticketing station. After pushing some buttons, she had a solution.

"Your train is departing from platform twenty-one and it will be leaving in about ten minutes. You need new tickets. You better hurry or you will miss it." With haste, she printed our new tickets and handed them over. Turns out, the train that was posted on the schedule didn't exist. We were supposed to get on that first train that arrived at platform twenty-one with the name of a town we didn't recognize. Talk about confusing. Quickly, we ran to the train at platform twenty-one and hopped on. Praying it would take us back to Dolo. Nervously, we sat in our seats hoping for familiar landmarks. Once outside of Venice, we started to recognize town names and knew we were on the right train—half an hour late, but the right train. We settled into our seats, relaxed and enjoyed the view as we headed back to visit with our newfound Italian friend.

Guido's place is set up like a small farm complete with chickens. One evening, a chicken didn't make its way back into the coop in time. Darryl and I sat and watched it from under the oak tree as we waited for Guido to join us. Round and round it walked and squawked, searching for a way into the coop with its other chicken friends.

"I think you have a rogue chicken," I pointed out to Guido as he happily brought out another bottle of limoncello.

"Yes. It is always the same one. You help." He motioned to Darryl for assistance in bringing the rebel chicken into the coop. Darryl isn't a farmer in the least so it was quite comical watching Darryl taking orders from Guido on how and when to open the chicken coop gate. Guido herded the bird around the coop and Darryl opened the gate just in time to save the day. Mrs. Chicken was now happy and safe with the rest of the brood.

Those unique evenings at Guido's house were the highlight of the Italian portion of our trip. How fantastic it was to get to know Guido and learn about his heritage. I never thought I could sit and communicate with a stranger who speaks a different language into the wee hours of the morning. Of course, maybe the limoncello made our Italian better and Guido's English sharper as well.

"My great-great aunt lived in this house." Guido had a story to share. "It was said she killed her husband. Knocked him on the head with a frying pan." At least that's what appliance we think he said. "Whack." Guido made a motion with his hand as if he were delivering the fatal blow. "Kaput." Guido clapped his hands together twice in a sweeping motion making a clap-clap sound. "Nobody could prove it. Body was never found. She was free." Who would have thought we would be privy to a hundred-year-old Italian murder mystery.

We connected. We bonded. To this day we still hear from Guido. He sends us pictures of events in Venice and we messaged him when Venice flooded to see if he was alright. He was far enough away from the floods, so all was well. It was a reason for us to reach out and say, "Hi, we are thinking about you on the other side of the world." Guido lives the good life and he shared his culture with us in a personal way. *How cool is that?*

Chapter 15

Italy's Alps

Prior to our exploration trip, I had never been away from home for more than two weeks. Homesickness was starting to settle in. We had been away from home for nearly a month when we reached Sestriere.

We have a timeshare that we sometimes use for an exchange (if you want to buy a timeshare, I have one to sell you). There was a week available in Sestriere, an alpine village in Metropolitan Turin. It is 17 kilometres from the border of France. Sestriere was a little further out of Turin than we would have liked but we needed to use the timeshare. I'm glad we did.

Until this time, I had thought Canada's Rocky Mountains were unparalleled in their beauty. I was wrong. The Italian Alps bare a remarkable resemblance to our Rockies, which was medicine for my soul. The view we had from our room in Sestriere was the cure I required for my homesickness. Lonely thoughts flowed away as soon as I stepped onto the balcony to see God's glorious creation. A massive, rocky mountain with a touch of snow in the craggy valleys peered back at me from its lofty perch. Pine trees climbed halfway up the sides, the higher elevations too harsh a climate for anything to survive. Green meadows and trees surrounded the mountain like an ocean of jade. Cowbells rang in the distance. The air smelled fresh and pure like after a spring rain. Children laughed gleefully while they played soccer at a school near the town centre. They were tiny ants from our view, but their laughter carried to our ears on the crisp mountain air. This would be our view every night and every morning for the next seven days. *What a gift.*

I love the outdoors. Put me outside any time of the day and I am content. Humans were not created to sit at a desk all day, staring at a computer screen, straining their eyes to the point of exhaustion. Humans were created to be in the garden. Our design is to explore the great outdoors and tend to the allotment we have been gifted with. People have gravitated to the big cities and so we have lost much of our oneness with nature. The excitement of the city is alluring but is it also draining. It can chew you up and spit you out. Perhaps even swallow you entirely. *Is the breakdown of our social lives and instincts a cause of the chaos pressed upon us by a big city?*

At one time, I felt a gravitational pull to an office job. I wanted to climb the corporate ladder. I was sure I could handle the pressure. Being promoted and earning more money with each new job was my definition of success. What I didn't realize was how a desk job would stifle my creativity. How it was a prison where I sold my time to someone in exchange for a wage. It wasn't until I got laid off that I realized nobody cared about the work I did. I was replaceable and it didn't matter how special I thought I was or how hard I worked. There was so much more to experiencing life than sitting in an office all day getting more and more stressed out, miserable and hating my job.

"Yo, relax," is my son's favourite saying and now finally we had the chance to do just that. I am not a stationary person. I like to be moving. Sitting at a beach is not a vacation for me. I get bored and I need to explore. Travel is like being a two-year old again. When we travel, I can't wait to get out of bed in the morning. In Sestriere, there were castles and fortresses to explore. Driving through the mountains on the hairpin turns as we headed for our next destination was exhilarating. Even just the sound of the church bells ringing every fifteen minutes to signal the time passing filled me with joy. I love the sound of the church bells ringing through the countryside and through the small towns. I wonder if the residents even notice them anymore.

Travel is my opportunity to discover this world and expand my intelligence as I am constantly learning while travelling, not only about the destination but about myself and other cultures. Food is a significant part of other cultures. Even how restaurants operate is different in Europe. In Italy, the small family owned restaurants in the tiny towns don't have a menu. We would approach a restaurant to see an 8 ½ x 11 piece of paper with the menu of the day sketched out in handwriting. Usually, the meal consisted of three courses. A pasta entrée to start followed by the main dish of meat and a vegetable. Then a dessert to sweeten us up. Sometimes coffee was included and wine was always involved. Water would be an extra charge. These special three course menus were usually priced at €10 or C$14. Not bad for all the fixings.

As we would walk under the trees, we would hear the cicadas sing. Cicadas are ugly looking bugs that look like a cross between a giant green fly, grasshopper and monster from outer space. The sound of the cicadas can sometimes be deafening. Most prevalent in Rome, the dastardly singing bugs stay high up in the trees making a grating, chirping type sound ten times as loud as a common Canadian cricket. I love these new experiences. They bring balance back to my mind and body as I observe, learn and relax at the same time. No distractions. No TV. No internet. No phones ringing. No radio.

Some coffee and reading in the morning and then we were off to explore ancient fortresses and mountain towns. France was so close so we took a day trip to Briançon, a small town in southern France close to the Italian border. We wandered the streets of the walled portion of the city and decided to head to the Fort du Chateau. Construction of the medieval fort took place in the 14th century. At an altitude of 1395 metres, the fort was considered the highest city in Europe at one point in time.

Darryl's lungs were not faring well with the high altitude. As we walked up to the entrance of the upper fort, he barged forward, head down, and kept walking up the stairs. He was on a mission. He knew if he stopped, he wouldn't make it. There was a young man in his early twenties standing behind a table with brochures spread out in front of him.

"Monsieur! Monsieur!" It was not free to go beyond that point. I knew that but Darryl had chosen to forget this tiny detail.

"Darryl, stop," I called out curtly. "It's not free. You have to pay."

"I'm not going then." He muttered in disgust. When Darryl isn't feeling well, his patience runs short.

"Fine. You can sit down here and enjoy the view. I'll go on my own." I paid my €5, got my guidebook and proceeded to explore. I enjoyed myself thoroughly taking in the astonishing views of the French Alps. It was windy at the top. My hair was blowing everywhere, making selfies a challenge, especially for a selfie-challenged person like me. I took my time. After all, Darryl needed his rest. About forty-five minutes later, I made my way back down. Just outside the entrance to the fort, sat my darling, dedicated husband. All by himself perched on a rock under the only tree on the hillside. He looked so cute sitting there, patiently waiting for his lady. The lovely town of Briançon a picturesque backdrop behind him. The mountains, blue sky and fluffy white clouds, the perfect frame for my knight in shining armour.

Europe has such an incredible advantage with so many countries being so close together. When you near bordering countries, you can see the cultures melding by the architecture and the names of the towns. The town of Lille in northern France is right along the Belgium border. The architecture in Lille is distinctly Flemish Renaissance Revival style with interesting stepped silhouettes on the rooftops. In northern Italy, towns such as Exilles and Fenestrelle are now Italian but their names are distinctly French. Historically, the towns were part of France but now lie within Italian borders. Many Italian towns had French names because of former borders from long ago. English was not widely spoken in the area. Most people spoke both French and Italian. We wished we had paid better attention in French class back in grade school. I took French from grades three to ten; you'd think I would be fluent but I'm not. Hindsight is 20/20.

Note to Self: Learn a new language, or at least
brush up on the French you learned so long ago.

The beautiful little town of Sestriere set the mood for the remainder of our time in Europe. No longer would we rush from place to place. We would stay longer, relax and enjoy the transformation we were beginning to see in each other. Driving in Italy taught me patience and tolerance. Correction—being a passenger in Italy taught me patience and tolerance. I had nearly flown off the handle at Darryl a couple of times during harrowing driving experiences. Such as driving up a street in San Gimignano because we wanted a closer parking spot only to find ourselves inside the town walls where you shouldn't be driving. Up one street we went until it became too narrow so we had to travel in reverse all the way back down. What a terrifying, not to mention, awkward experience. Now, I would calmly say, "Well, just back down, no problem." I have learned to keep my emotions in check and focus on solving the problem rather than reacting to it.

Chapter 16

Austria

Where in the world is Abtenau? We had never heard of this alpine town before but it was coming up in our search for accommodations outside Salzburg. The population of Abtenau is just over fifty-seven hundred. Salzburg was out of the question for our budget so we decided on an inn located in the sleepy town of Abtenau. Placing the address in the GPS, we made our way through the glorious Austrian Alps. I had no idea Austria had mountains like they did. They too rivalled the Canadian Rockies in their rugged beauty and soaring heights.

We arrived in Abtenau by mid-afternoon. Another celebrated sunny day with clear skies was given to us. The GPS would not be so kind, though. We could not find the house number of our hotel so I chose the number next in sequence. Obviously, our destination would be right next to the address I had chosen.

The typical gabled houses with flower boxes adorning the windows rolled up the hillsides in the mountain valley. Despite its quaint size, the town had a centre and then spread out in two different directions. One direction up the mountain and the other direction toward Salzburg. Our GPS took us up the mountainous side of the market town to an address that was a house with no hotels in sight. I had saved a picture of the exterior of the hotel on my phone so we knew what the building looked like. Nothing in sight even came close to resembling our destination. I had also taken a snapshot of Google maps and the town so if we did get lost, we had a map to figure out where we were in case there was no Wi-Fi.

Darryl and I studied the map and realized we must be in the completely wrong area of town. Based on the map, our hotel was on the other side of Abtenau, down the hill toward Salzburg. *How was this possible?* So, we drove down the main road with no success. We drove the other direction, apprehension kicking in.

"There it is," I cried out, as I pointed out the window to the same inn that was gracing the screen of my phone. Darryl pulled into the barren parking lot.

"Is this place even open?" Darryl asked with trepidation. There was no one around on this property at the very edge of town.

"I guess we will find out." We both got out of the car and went to the front door. It was locked.

"There is another door by the patio," I said. We headed over and walked inside. A man with short blonde, spiked hair and glasses walked up to us. He was of average height and weight with face piercings and tattoos. He was dressed in brown leather lederhosen. I didn't think people wore lederhosen anymore. I was wrong.

"Hello," he said nonchalantly.

"Are you open?" I asked.

"Yes." Another one-word response without expression.

"We have reservations. Can we check in?"

"Yes." He continued to look at me. *This dude is weird,* I thought. *Where is the reciprocity in communication?* He wasn't doing anything. Just standing there with a deadpan look on his face. I put my hands up and opened my palms in a questioning motion as if to say, *Well… Are you going to help us or not?*

"Come with me." He turned around and started walking to another room. We followed.

"My name is Jakob." Once he started the check-in process, he became conversational. A large, barking Rottweiler welcomed us into the lobby along with the overpowering smell of wet dog.

"She is fine," Jakob said plainly, "The front door is always locked. Please lock it behind you when you leave. Here is your key." Once again, I was starting to doubt the reviews on our hotel site.

Jakob took us up to our room. It was dated but would suffice for a couple of nights. The bathroom had a faint smell of an old urinal but it appeared clean. This place was in need of upgrades.

"Jakob, we had troubles finding this hotel. It wouldn't show up on our GPS and the address next door took us to the other side of town." Darryl quizzed our host about the odd address.

"Oh, yes. Well, in Abtenau, the addresses do not go in sequence. The addresses are given to the properties at the time they are built. So, the address that you went to was built just before this inn." A matter-of-fact statement from a matter-of-fact type of guy.

Note to Self: Classic. Triple check any address we will be staying at from now on with the booking site, Google and any pictures available.

Jakob turned out to be a wealth of information on seeing sights in Salzburg; however, he didn't have much to suggest about Abtenau. "Please, please, please, if you find any nightlife in Abtenau, come back and tell me." Apparently, Jakob needed to get out more often.

Jakob showed us on a map where to find an affordable place to park when we visited Salzburg. Too bad we couldn't find it.

The only one we kept coming across was the expensive parking garage he told us to avoid. We opted to park there anyway rather than continue to drive around. It was underground in a select location close to everything we wanted to see.

Eating was always on our minds so after exploring the main square, we headed off on a side street to get some food. As usual, it took us passing about three establishments before we could agree on one we both wanted to eat at. There was no one outside on the small patio so I walked in the open door. A petite elderly lady with a grandmotherly smile came to me. "Do you speak English?" I asked. She shook her head no. "Can we sit outside?" I motioned to a table outside since she said she couldn't speak English. She nodded an enthusiastic yes.

The restaurant was a Polish restaurant and my guess was the grandmother was the sole cook and owner. We ordered a dark beer, true to our nature. Darryl ordered meatloaf and potatoes. I ordered Hunter's stew. The beer grandma brought out was as black as ebony with a tan-coloured creamy head. Our eyes lit up. This looked good. I took the first drink.

"You are going to love this," I exclaimed to Darryl. The beer was one of the best I've tasted. It was a Polish beer called 1881 Porter. I have never seen it anywhere since. The beer was deep and rich with a hint of coffee, chocolate and licorice. It was super smooth, even with a 9.5% alcohol volume.

"That is good." Darryl was in heaven. We finished about half our beer by the time the food came. Darryl got what he ordered but I'm pretty sure I did not. On my plate was a round hunk of meat that appeared to be a giant ground beef-type meatball. It was covered in a smooth tomato sauce resembling Campbell's Tomato Soup. A sprinkling of green onions adorned the dish to add some colour. *Oh well, she can't speak English. I'll eat it anyway.* It turned out to be tasty.

While we were eating, another English couple came on to the patio and were met by Grandma. "Do you speak English?" The man asked. They got the same response we did—she shook her head no. So, they left and went to the restaurant right beside us. *What was that? Talk about rude.* Darryl and I looked at each other, astonished that someone would leave a restaurant when the server didn't speak English. *You are in Austria, remember?*

When we were done our meals, Grandma cleared the table and brought us out a pretty little silver tray with two shot glasses on it. The liquid was golden in colour. "Polish Vodka," Grandma announced with a smile. She nodded and left our table. I guess she can speak English when alcohol is involved. We didn't order this but what the heck, maybe it was a gift from her to us. So, we drank it. The beverage was smooth and slightly sweet, very tasty as well. A perfect finish. But Grandma wasn't done yet.

Next came out dessert. A beautiful cake with a berry bottom, white cake centre and meringue topping. A yellow sauce was poured over the top and blueberries sprinkled on the cake and plate. She motioned to me to eat and patted me on the shoulder. I hadn't ordered this but apparently, she thought I needed more meat on my bones because Darryl wasn't offered a piece. *How could I say no?* Down went the cake and it was as flavoursome as it looked. The bill came and it turns out Grandma was the master of the upsell. Cake and Polish Vodka were not free. We paid with cash, not expecting change, and of course, she did not return with any. Now I think I know why the other visitors left when she said she didn't speak English. Perhaps they had this experience once too. Honestly, Darryl and I didn't mind. It was part of the encounter and we had fun. I'd go back and see Granny again.

Note to Self: Never underestimate sweet, little old ladies.

Filled with Polish delights, Darryl and I made our way back to Mozartplatz for further exploration of Salzburg. Something was up. A heavy police presence had descended on the square since our visit before lunch.

"I wonder what's going on?" Darryl said quizzically.

"Maybe someone famous is coming." I was excited. We had been surprised in Jerash, Jordan with an unexpected visit to the site by Prince William and the Crown Prince of Jordan, Hussein bin Abdullah. *Who would grace our presence this time?* Anticipation began to build in the air. More police showed up, standing on the outskirts of the square. A large crowd began to congregate in the centre of the square. Young people in their early twenties began to show up as well, their rainbow-coloured hair made them easy to distinguish. They were here for a different purpose. They wore jean jackets, chains and tattoos. Explicit language was printed on the back of some of their jackets. *Maybe things will could get out of hand.* I thought. *Should we leave? No way.*

By this point, Darryl and I realized no one famous was showing up. We were in the middle of a pro-life rally. The people in the centre were carrying white crosses and banners. The small amount of protestors with multi-coloured hair began to get agitated. Two of the women started singing songs in German, directing their voices at the pro-life demonstrators. I couldn't understand exactly what they were singing but it was along the lines of "Let us abort." They started another round of singing and an overweight girl burst out in a coughing fit. Very classy.

An elderly man carrying a white wooden cross over his shoulder approached the group of young-people protestors that were close to us on the sidewalk. His finger was pointed at them and you could tell he was giving a lecture. The young men with multi-coloured hair crossed their arms in defiance, but they never assaulted the man. Once the old man was done his reprimand, he handed out pamphlets to the young girls in the protestors' circle, which they quickly tore up and threw on the ground.

My body was tingling with excitement and a bit of fear. You could feel the tension in the air. It was thick with anger and hostility. Darryl and I watched from the sidelines as the police moved to the centre of the square and surrounded the pro-life group. It was time for the march for life to start. Slowly, the group with their signs and crosses began exiting the square, surrounded by Salzburg's finest for protection. The ring-leader of the protestors approached the pro-life group and that's when the police took action. One police officer put on his gloves, and with a stern look on his face that exuded authority, daring them to "Bring it on." There was sudden commotion with the ring-leader and the police. Quickly, the police took the ring-leader of the protestors to the ground, hand-cuffed her and took her away. The speedy reaction of the police turned off the rest of the protestors and the pro-life group moved forward without further incident. The protestors dispersed and so did we; unscathed, thank goodness.

Eventually, we made our way back to the car. There was a problem, though. When Darryl turned on the car and I went to put the address in the GPS, everything was in French. The car had reverted to its original settings. *Did this happen because we were underground?* We had already paid our parking fee so we had a minimal time to get out of the parking garage.

"Just drive and I'll get it figured out," I said to Darryl. One thing Italy had taught me was to roll with the punches when you are in a vehicle. Don't panic. Keep going around the roundabout until you get to the right exit. Everything will turn out okay. I fiddled with the GPS while Darryl drove.

"I'm sure I can get it back to English. Just hang on," I said with determination in my voice. Finally, I found the settings to change the language. The first country that came up on the list was Australia so I selected that one and put in our address for Abtenau.

We discovered a demure lady with an Australian accent would be our next guide as we heard, "Enter the roundabout." *What happened to the cheery lady with a British accent?*

"Change it. Find the other voice." Panic filled Darryl's tone.

"Why? What's wrong with this one?"

"What if Australians have a different way of saying turn left?" He was deadly serious.

"She is speaking English, Darryl." I started to giggle.

"I don't care. Find the other voice." He was not amused at my humour.

"Fine," I muttered through a smile. After more searching, I found the cheery British lady again, much to Darryl's relief. We made it back to Abtenau without further incident. It would not be the last time our car malfunctioned.

Chapter 17

Dark History

"Arbeit Macht Frei." A lie etched in the metal gates of Dachau Concentration Camp in Germany. Once you saw those words and the inside of those black, cold metal gates, you knew freedom was gone. "Work Will Set You Free." Only one of the many deceits bestowed upon the people of Nazi Germany.

Visiting Dachau Concentration Camp was the most sobering experience on our trip to Europe. Dachau was our first stop in Germany after leaving Austria. We opted to take the English guided tour of the camp in order to get a full understanding of the dark history hovering over the small town of Dachau.

It was hot and dry on the day of our visit with no breeze to offer relief. Our tour began at 2:00 p.m. and was scheduled to last an hour. It was a fair-sized group of about twelve people. We all waited patiently in the lobby of the canteen for our guide to arrive. Some of us were more patient than others. There was a teenage boy complaining to his father about going on an hour-long tour. His whining was irritating. *Do you think the people brought to this camp eighty-five years ago wanted to be held captive here? Have some respect.*

Dachau was the first concentration camp built by the Nazis during their occupation. It was opened on March 22, 1933 for political prisoners, those Hitler deemed to be a threat to his dictatorship. The camp would become the training grounds for the SS (the Schutzstaffel), Hitler's private thugs posing as police. The first person to make the list into Dachau was a Jewish lawyer, who had once questioned Hitler on the stand in a court of law and caused Hitler to stutter. This humiliated Hitler and stirred up hatred beyond comprehension for the lawyer. Cross Hitler, and your name would be added to the infamous list.

Dachau was a camp strictly for male prisoners. In 1935, the Nuremberg Laws were passed allowing racial discrimination. New prisoner groups would now be sent to Dachau. Anyone who did not fit into Hitler's master plan would be imprisoned, including immigrants, priests, Jehovah's Witnesses, and homosexuals. The camp was constructed to house six thousand prisoners. All these people were left to the vices of the SS, who could treat the prisoners in any manner they pleased.

The SS was Hitler's creation and literally meant "Protection Squadron." A dictator's mob squad available to secure and dispose of those Hitler perceived to be his enemies. You had to apply to be a member of the SS and you were also interviewed to make sure you fit the qualifications. Our guide was excellent in explaining all angles of the story. She said it was considered an honour back then to be a part of the SS. The men were paid well and they were given nice, shiny uniforms. They felt important. The SS did not live inside the concentration camp but adjacent to it in the officer's barracks. They were fed well and had clean living conditions. It was there they would also be brainwashed into hate. Dachau was to become the model of all concentration camps in Nazi Germany.

There are pictures of the first prisoners who arrived at the camp in the museum at Dachau. Former prison barracks display a vast number of pictures of prisoners, some enduring torture, and survivors of the camp. There was a picture of the first prisoners as they entered the camp. They looked defeated, save one man who stood up tall in his prison uniform in direct defiance of the SS leading him into Dachau. He did not survive.

The soldiers did not need any reason to choose someone to be the object of their misdeeds. If you didn't make your bed right, they could torture you. If you did make your bed right, they would mess it up and then torture you. The preferred method of torment was to tie a man's hands behind his back and then hoist him up and hang him from the ceiling by his wrists. This could go on for hours. If the prisoner passed out, he would be revived. Other experiments would be to inject air into men's veins to see how they would react to an embolism. There are pictures of these experiments in the museum. Those images burnt into my brain and still haunt me.

The priests in the camps were particularly hated by the Nazis. However, there was one prisoner respected above all others by both the prisoners and the guards. Our guide went on to tell us about this brave man who was given the task of leading a team of priests to build a new structure at Dachau. This structure of brick was not inside the camp fences. It was hidden beyond the fences, in the trees, out of sight.

Word of gas chambers had reached the prisoners of the camp. Gas chambers were not in the initial plans of Dachau but the Nazis had to come up with a more efficient way for their killing machine. Once the priests realized they were being forced to build a gas chamber, they slowed their efforts, taking an exceedingly long time to complete this building. When the leader of the SS confronted the team lead as to why it was taking so long, the man responded, "What did you expect? You gave me priests to build it!" *What a story of boldness.* The gas chamber at Dachau was never used.

"Did the people of Dachau know what was going on?" Someone asked our guide during the tour.

"Yes. There was no way they couldn't know what was going on inside the camp. But we cannot be quick to judge. We have no idea what it was like living under a dictatorship. They knew if they spoke up, they would be behind these walls. They were told, and believed, the people behind these walls were criminals. Some felt they deserved to be here because of their so-called crimes. It is not an excuse for their actions. It means we don't understand." After the Allies liberated the camp, they forced the people of Dachau to walk through the facilities to see what was going on in their backyards. Dachau residents were forced to clean up the horrors to which they had turned a blind and fearful eye.

The most poignant memorial at Dachau was an abstract of metal. A statue of people molded together to look like a barbed-wire fence sits in front of the prison buildings. The significance of the people on the fence is in remembrance of those who chose death by grabbing the electric fences surrounding the camp rather than suffering further agonies.

Only the foundations remain of the original barracks. A row of trees stretches along the main road in the camp square. Trees planted by the prisoners, by force, to be a façade of well-being on the grounds. Now, the trees are full-grown and stand as a testament in all their greenery to the lives lost and saved. It is a whisper of life where at one time there was only death. I could picture the prisoners digging holes to plant the trees, dressed in their striped, dirty prison garb, wiping their brows in the blistering heat.

"I will end the tour here," said our guide as we arrived at the gas chamber and crematorium. "Most people don't want to go inside so I will leave you to explore the area as you are comfortable." The guide and some people left. We stayed.

It is surreal to stand at the doors leading into the rectangular building built for such horrors. Darryl and I entered the rooms where people disrobed and prepared for their showers. Clothing was disinfected and fumigated in this area.

"Brausebad." The word above the showers evoked fear into people. To this day, it still conjures up a feeling of despair and dread. The gas chamber was square, cold and dark. Horrifying. Just like the rest of the camp. Everything was built in square angles to force a sense of monotony.

There were two death rooms in the building, one on each side of the crematorium. Death rooms were used to store corpses for disposal. Also, the SS would not stoop so low as to do the dirty work. Prisoners were forced to carry the dead to be incinerated and stack them like logs in the death rooms. The prisoners were also the ones to place the bodies in the ovens for incineration. It was a form of mental torture to make the men dispose of the bodies. Their comrades. Their friends.

Death room 2. I entered this room next to the crematorium in silence. Everyone in the building was still. It was too much to comprehend the suffering. *How could people do this to their fellow human beings? How could hate grow to such extreme levels?* As I stood there, looking around the empty, square room, the church bells rang to signal the top of the hour. Emotion welled up inside me and I could not help myself. I cried.

I had to get out of that room. Stepping outside into the sunshine, tears rolling down my face, I took a deep breath and wiped my tears away. I put my sunglasses back on to hide my emotional reaction. I needed a few minutes to compose myself on a bench outside. Darryl came and sat beside me in silence. Once we got a grip on ourselves, we got up and continued to look around the area and pay our respects to people buried in the mass graves.

Once the Allies had a stronghold on Nazi Germany, Hitler's plan was to blow up all the concentration camps with the prisoners still inside the walls to hide the evidence. At the height of Nazi rule, there were over thirty thousand concentration camps throughout the countries suffering Germany's occupation. Slowly, the Allies liberated all the camps, some prisoners rushing out excited and dying at the same time from malnutrition. US Army troops liberated thirty-two thousand prisoners from Dachau on April 29, 1945.

Our guide said school groups come to Dachau on field trips. The Germans feel it is important for the young generation to know what their ancestors did. Important so the tragedy never happens again. I agree with this and I also agree that it is important for tourists to visit these sites. Only through education can we prevent these terrible atrocities from happening again. Refusing to visit sites such as Dachau is equivalent to putting your head in the sand. It is wrong to cover up the past and pretend it didn't happen. Travel is not just about having fun. It is about education and making the world a better place. History is our greatest teacher.

A visit to Dachau Concentration Camp is not for the faint of heart, nor is it a place to take small children. It is a mass graveyard deserving of our respect. The surviving relatives have requested it be a memorial for the perished thousands. Thousands with no known grave, only graves of ashes.

Chapter 18

Germany

Germany is the Autobahn. You want to talk about stimulation? Ask Darryl what it felt like when we drove up the highway ramp toward a sign marked "Autobahn." Slight horror but total excitement. We had both always thought the Autobahn was a long stretch of one highway in Germany where speed limits didn't exist. This is not the case. *All* the highways in Germany are the Autobahn. No speed limits anywhere, unless posted. It's brilliant and Germans know how to drive. For the three weeks we spent in Germany, we saw no accidents on these highways of incredible speed. People don't cut you off. They respect the rules of the road and they respect other drivers. *Novel concept, don't you think?*

There are rules to driving the Autobahn and Darryl decided to learn them before we embarked on a whole new mind-bending adventure:

1. Slower traffic keep right. This does apply in North America, people, so for the love of God will you please start obeying it? It does work. So, get out of the way if you plan on driving the speed limit, or slower.

2. Semis and big trucks can drive in the far-right lane only.

3. The middle lane has an average speed of approximately 140 kilometres an hour. Don't worry, you can work your way up to it. Plus, it doesn't feel that fast when Lamborghini's are blowing by you in the fast lane at 200 kilometres an hour.

4. Passing is illegal on the right side. Don't do it. This is also marvelous as you don't have some yahoo flying by you on the right side, weaving in and out of traffic like a Tasmanian devil. A site that is oh, so common in North America.

5. Use the far-left lane to pass only. Unless you are driving 200 kilometres an hour, then chances are people need to get out of your way.

6. If someone starts blinking their headlights behind you, pull over to the right lane beside you. You are driving too slow and they are warning you to get out of the way. This also prevents the passing on the right-side insanity so prevalent in our driving culture.

7. If speeds are posted (sometimes they are) then drive the speed limit.

8. That's it! Now, have fun! You are about to embark on the Autobahn. Germany's most superb invention.

Note to Self: An unwritten rule of the Autobahn that has been drafted by crafty drivers — Wait until your wife falls asleep on the passenger side and then floor it. She'll never know.

By now you get it. The roads in Germany are magnificent. It has brought forth a different driving culture than what we have in Canada, and I don't mean just the speed. Canada is such a massive country and we are used to driving distances of 500 kilometres or more in a day, often without a second thought. Driving on the Autobahn requires such intense concentration by the driver that Germans drive far shorter distances.

We were staying in Ilmmünster, a small-town about 40 kilometres north of Munich. Our host was Paul, who spoke some English and was curious about our travelling style.

"Where are you headed today? Munich?" We were checking-out as we had explored some sights around the area and it was time to move on.

"No, we were in Munich yesterday. We are headed to Gemünd."

He looked confused. "Gemünd… by Düsseldorf? That is over 600 kilometres away. Driving that in one day?"

"Yes. We are used to driving far distances in one day." We went on to explain how big Canada was. Europeans have no concept of a single country that is so huge and how we can drive such vast distances in one day without batting an eye. The same goes for Canadians, we cannot fathom how far Europeans will walk or cycle in one day. It's their lifestyle. Part of the reason they can also eat so much bread.

"That's bullshit." He laughed. "We drive the most 250 kilometres in a day and that is enough." He shook his head, waved, and wished us safe travels.

We did break up our journey with a stop at Rothenburg ob der Tauber, the picturesque fairytale town you have probably seen pictures of and don't realize where it is. Germany is full of beautiful, walled medieval towns. I fell in love with Germany. My heritage is German and I could picture my relatives walking the cobblestone streets hundreds and thousands of years ago.

Germany is an incredibly affordable destination. Once we were settled in Gemünd we headed out for groceries. We were here for a week so I was anxious to see what treasures we could find at a German grocery store. We discovered that they don't refrigerate eggs in Europe. We found that odd and a little suspect so were hesitant to buy any, but we love eggs so thought, *well, if the Germans are alive and well eating them, we should be fine too.* The eggs came complete with the odd feather and a little bit of poo.

With my cart stocked for groceries for the week, we proceeded to the checkout. We had enough meat, produce and sauerkraut to keep us satisfied until we left. Add a bottle of wine, a six pack of beer and a bottle of whiskey and we were set. The grand total after all was said and done? €32. That's C$47. You can hardly buy a bottle of whiskey for that in Canada. I was going to like this country. *How could I buy groceries back home again and be satisfied?*

We took a day trip to Monschau from Gemünd. It was in this picture-perfect medieval town that I had my first wiener schnitzel. Since I was a child, I had always wanted to eat wiener schnitzel in Germany. I'm not sure why. I think I just liked the way it sounded. The wiener schnitzel was perfect. It arrived golden brown, crispy, and seasoned perfectly with a slice of lemon to drizzle over top. The dish was accompanied with fries and a salad but the wiener schnitzel was the star of the show. German food takes me back to childhood and Mom's home cooking. Comfort food at its finest. Sausages, mashed potatoes, gravy, spaetzle. My stomach is starting to growl. Simple ingredients to create delicious meals. That's what German food is all about.

Darryl and I also found we blended in with the people in Germany. We didn't feel as if we were tourists, partly because of our European heritage. We looked like we belonged in the country. People would come up to us and start talking in German and we would have to shrug our shoulders and say, "Do you speak English?" It took me almost a month to finally learn how to ask in German if the person spoke English.

Germany has everything. Beautiful scenery, especially in Bavaria with its glorious mountain ranges and castles. History galore with medieval villages and towns—Germany has done a remarkable job at maintaining their darling walled towns. Great food, and friendly people that know how to drive. Germany is an easy country to get around in.

Another day trip we took from Gemünd was to Cologne. First stop was the incredible Cologne Cathedral. The Gothic spires of the cathedral are amongst the tallest in the world at close to 175 metres. We parked underneath the towering cathedral. When I first stepped out and looked up what stood before me took my breath away. All I could see was the cathedral stretching up to the heavens. It looked like it was touching the clouds. The massive arches and spires reached upward and seemed to form into a triangle at the top. The building has survived bombings and world wars. It is a miracle it still stands.

I simply had to walk up to the top of this tower. Darryl was not so keen. Heights aren't his thing. He agreed to go halfway up so I left him in the middle and proceeded up the narrow stairwell. The air inside the stairwell was stifling. It was hot and smelled like a gym locker room. Stale sweat permeated the walls. I continued and 533 steps later, I was at the top with outstanding views of the city of Cologne in all directions. The maximum height to climb is 101 metres so there is still a tall spire that juts out above that you cannot reach. The walls inside were covered with graffiti. The perfect selfie-moment. I actually like the selfie in the cathedral tower. I am looking outside at the city and you can see the calmness in my face that isn't in earlier pictures. I'm not flushed from climbing the stairs but I have a lovely glow that radiates happiness. I took my time and didn't rush. I am living in the moment and it's apparent in my eyes.

We paid for our parking on the way back to the car. Our ten minutes to get out of the lot without an issue began ticking. It was hot inside the car, steaming hot, even though we were underground and out of the sun. Darryl put the keys in the ignition but nothing happened. The car was dead. He tried again. Nothing. No lights, no sounds, no bells, no British accent, nothing.

"What the—?" Darryl was perplexed. We tried everything. Taking the key in and out of the ignition, using the spare set, turning every dial and button we could see. Nothing. By this time, we had the doors wide open or we would have been slowly baked alive. We were starting to get concerned because we only had a few minutes left before our grace period to get out of the parking garage ended and we'd have to pay another fee. But, we were calmer people now, so we sat back to think.

"Let's get out of the car." I had an idea.

"Why?" Darryl looked at me quizzically.

"Let's try starting from the beginning. Get out and lock the doors. Then unlock them again with the key."

"Okay, if you say so."

Out we got and stood at the car as if we had just arrived. Darryl locked the doors. Waited a second and then unlocked them again.

"Okay, let's get back in and try this again." Calmly, we both got back in the car. With anticipation, Darryl put the key back in the ignition and turned the key. The car started purring like a kitten. *Go figure.*

Germany is where I discovered my niche for my travel blog. Part of the reason for us to go on this European excursion was to find that niche. What did we love about travelling and what could

I write about that was unique? I loved food, history, drink and taking photos but that wasn't narrow enough. Turns out, small towns are where I find inspiration.

On our last night in Germany, we decided to stay overnight in a castle in Waldeck. Schloss Waldeck is a castle converted into a four-star hotel. It was fantastic and the price was extremely reasonable. We paid just over C$200 for the night, which included a fabulous breakfast buffet overlooking the Edersee. The room was completely renovated and spacious. The bathroom was huge. Germany is an incredibly affordable destination so we could treat ourselves to one four-star night.

The restaurant was closed after lunch and we arrived a bit later so we headed into town to find a place to eat. We stumbled across a place simply signed as "Biergarten." At first, we weren't sure if it was open to the public since there were no people around and there seemed to be no name to this intriguing spot. It was quiet, but the gate was open, so we went inside and wandered around the terrace enjoying a spectacular view of the German countryside. A man came out to greet us. We asked if he spoke English.

"Nein," he shook his head.

"Can we sit here and eat?" Making motions with our hands to get our point across.

"Ja." We sat down and ordered beers, Jaeger schnitzel, salad and frites from the simple menu the man provided. He did his best to communicate and so did we. We sipped our beer and waited for our German culinary specialty to arrive.

It was just Darryl, myself and our view at this point in our lives. We drank in the moment. The air was hot and dry. The sky was azure blue painted with slight wisps of white cloud. The summer had been unseasonably hot in Germany so the wheat fields were ripe and ready for harvesting. The yellow fields painted a stark contrast with the lush, green trees. The quiet village of lower Waldeck, with its white buildings and red and brown rooftops, seemed to sleep on this calm afternoon. It was at this place I realized how fast-paced we lived our lives back in Canada. *Why don't we take more time to sit with our loved ones and enjoy time? We rush from daily activities and don't reflect on our mortality. Just to sit, talk, and be.* It was there in the small German town, at an obscure Biergarten, where I realized this was what I wanted to write about. These experiences where all that exists in the world is yourself and the ones you love. The times we travel, forget about the hectic world back home, and realize there is more to life. Small-towns offered us the most relaxed experiences where we could immerse ourselves in the true culture and history of the countries we visited.

Our food arrived and we slowly enjoyed our meal. Taking our time with the view, the food and the beer. We paid in cash and our host gave us a handwritten receipt on a coloured piece of paper. It doesn't get much simpler than that.

Getting off the Autobahn and driving winding country roads to Waldeck was a turning point in our travels. The speed limit on life is slower in these small towns and it forces you to reflect on where you are going. How much more interesting and enjoyable our lunch in Waldeck was as we gazed at the countryside, alone. It was our last day in Germany. The next day we would be off to France for a short visit before we met up with Darryl's family in Belgium. Waldeck was the perfect end to our German adventure.

Chapter 19

Don't Mess with a Canadian

While looking for a place to stay in France, we came across an apartment with fantastic reviews in Lille, a town near the Belgian border. The overall rating of this flat had a number in the high nines. The place was "absolutely fabulous!" Based on the reviews, and pictures of the apartment, we chose this location over another.

Note to Self: Don't believe everything you read—unless of course, it's in this book.

Communication with the owner of the flat was good prior to our arrival. Pepe, sent us one communication stating that because of our status in a certain program, we would receive a complimentary beer or wine upon arrival and to let him know our choice. *A welcome gift? How delightful.* I responded to Pepe's email and said my husband liked beer and I liked wine and we looked forward to meeting him soon.

We arrived at the flat and Pepe was waiting for us. He was a man in his early fifties with dark slicked back hair and glasses. He greeted us warmly and handed us a blue parking disk we could display in our car to prevent a parking ticket.

"Don't worry if you get a ticket. I work for the police and will just cancel it." Pepe's breath smelled like stale cigarettes and burnt coffee.

We continued up to the apartment for our walk-through. When I say we continued up, I mean we continued way up. The apartment was on the fourth floor with tremendously narrow steps and no elevator. We are in good health, so this was not an issue for us, but what about people who can't climb stairs? This inconvenience was not mentioned in the listing. It was a real pain to carry luggage up the four flights of stairs. Also, the lighting was incredibly poor so it was a struggle to navigate our way through the halls to find the light switches so we could illuminate the way to our apartment door.

The apartment itself was clean; however, awfully small. The kitchen was so tiny that a mouse could hardly turn around in it. There was no countertop space. Preparing a meal would have been next to impossible. The kitchen was well stocked with items and cooking utensils but it was just not practical for use. The table area was fine for toast and coffee in the morning. There was a small sitting area with a television. The bed was located adjacent to the sitting area. The sleeping area was also tiny. Darryl would later find that the simple act of getting in and out of bed would result in his head hitting the walls. The windows opened inward. I had to duck underneath them when they were open in order to get around the bed. The bathroom was clean and exceptionally well stocked, it even came with condoms. *Ooh, la la.* That was a first.

Outside the apartment, a screeching noise from the tram ran right outside our window every ten minutes. That was going to be annoying and disruptive to my much-needed beauty sleep.

As we settled in to spend our first night at the apartment, I noticed our complimentary bottle of beer and wine was not in the fridge. I emailed Pepe to inquire and he promptly replied because we were not members of the special program we did not qualify for the gift. He also said prior arrangements had not been made to provide the beverages. *Interesting. I guess he didn't get my email.*

Well no big deal, we had some drinks with us anyway from Germany.

Our stay in the apartment was a short one, two nights to be exact, and for that we were grateful. After the other fabulous flats and pensions we had stayed at, this was by far our least favourite. It was just too small for our needs. Yes, it was clean, and cleanliness is the most important feature. We just didn't like the place or the location.

Our time in France had come to an end. We packed up, locked up, and headed to our car. A few steps after locking the front door and depositing the keys in the mailbox, I turned to Darryl and said, "We still have the blue parking disk in our car. Oh well, can't do anything about it now so I'll message Pepe to see where to mail it when we get to Belgium."

Throughout our travels, we had faithfully filled out the review requests sent to us by the websites we booked through. To stay true, we completed an honest feedback report on the room we stayed at in Lille, France. Our final rating came to an overall of 7.1, which we felt was not bad. Pepe didn't agree.

A few days later, we received a message from Pepe via communications through the booking site we used, "I am a little pissed off at the bad review you gave me." *Wait. What?* Pepe was taking this personal. He went on to say we were only mad because he didn't give us the beer and wine and our conduct was not what he expected from Canadians. He also accused us of stealing his blue parking disk.

Well, Pepe, now you have pissed off a Canadian. We were sitting in our relatives' garden in Belgium enjoying a beer when we received the email. Darryl and I were both shocked. *Did he just swear at us, insult us as Canadians, and accuse us of theft? Who responds to a customer's review in that tone? This guy must have brass balls.* After the shock wore off, our blood began to boil. What nerve. Body temperatures rose. A discussion erupted with our relatives about the ignorance of Pepe's email. Voices cracked with anger and disbelief. Heartbeats grew faster. Consensus was reached that Pepe was out of line. His conduct had to be addressed.

The next morning, with shaking hands, I sat down to write my response. I took the night to cool off so I would respond rationally. The email was frank and honest. If he can't take criticism, maybe he shouldn't be in the hospitality industry. His reaction to our review was uncalled for and not the way a businessman should treat customers. The unprofessional behaviour was reported to the booking site we used. Pepe responded again. Wasting time bantering back and forth would do no good. I ignored him. He wasn't worth any more energy. Returning shot for shot with this guy would only fuel the fire. *Goodbye, Pepe. I hope you are happier with your next review.*

Chapter 20

The Joy of Food

My watch had stopped working back in Egypt. A new battery was all I needed. I have worn a watch since junior high school and have been obsessed with time ever since. Always watching the clock and keeping myself on a tight schedule was how I kept my life in a constant state of orderly chaos. Constantly looking at my watch was driving me crazy and I didn't even realize it. By the time we arrived in Belgium three months later, I still had not replaced the battery in my watch. I have not replaced it to this day. I no longer needed to view my watch every five minutes to make sure I was on time. It didn't matter. I was in Europe now and the way the Europeans view time is completely different than the way Canadians view time. They take time to smell the roses, enjoying life and all it has to offer.

Darryl's grandmother came to Canada from Belgium in 1947. Many relatives are still in Belgium so this was our chance to spend time with them and immerse ourselves in Flemish culture. Darryl's family welcomed us with open arms, broad smiles, and plenty of kisses. We stayed with Ludo and Christiane, a delightful couple we had much in common with, despite our differences in age. Darryl had told me to be ready for kisses. Upon arrival, Ludo gave me a kiss on the right cheek and then the left. I thought we were done but he stated, "No. No. In Belgium we give three." *Alright. Three it is.* At first, kissing as a greeting felt awkward since our greetings are so cold in Canada, especially with new acquaintances. If we leaned in to kiss someone in Canada once, let alone three times, the person on the receiving end would think we were nuts. The situation might even end up with a slap. After a week in Belgium, we grew used to the special greeting. I would say we even came to like it. So much so, that we missed this ritual upon our return to Canada.

Note to Self: Not everyone in Belgium kisses three times. Sometimes twice is sufficient. Pay attention to the lead of the Belgian and follow suit.

Our stay with them lasted four weeks and we hoped we weren't overstaying our welcome. I am sure Ludo and Christiane were also wondering what in the world they would do with us for so long. I assured them we were easy to get along with and did not expect to be waited on. Plus, we had our own car so we could come and go as we pleased. They knew they were more than welcome to come along with us on an adventure or not. We got along smashingly.

"Charlotte got up and poured herself a glass of wine. That's when I knew everything would be okay," stated Ludo. We made ourselves at home and spent many wonderful evenings enjoying wine and brandy while visiting with Ludo and Christiane. Google translate was helpful when we couldn't find the right words to communicate.

Our second week into Belgium and I noticed my clothes were starting to get a little snug. A fat roll had also emerged that had not been there for a decade. Belgians love food and they love beer. Unfortunately, so do I. Because we were no longer cooking for ourselves, we were eating many things we didn't usually eat, and a lot more of it too. The food was wonderful and so were the beverages. If you have never had Belgian beer, do yourself a favour and buy one. I recommend Rochefort 10, my favourite. It is expensive in Canada but it is worth it, for a treat. It has become the beer I use to compare all beers.

Belgium arguably has the best beer in the world. Beer is woven into Belgian culture. So much so, the beer culture in Belgium was recognized as an Intangible Cultural Heritage by UNESCO. There are over 150 breweries in the tiny country with more than one thousand different Belgian beer brands. Once you have had a Belgian beer, you will never look at beer the same way again. Beer is readily available and it is common to have one in the afternoon. "Sandwich in a Glass" is a term the Belgians use—and it is appropriate. The beer is often thick enough to fill you up until dinner time. *Is it snack time yet?*

We were invited to homes for barbeques, birthday parties and anniversaries. It was an honour and a delight to meet all the relatives. I have never been to barbeques quite like how the Belgians host them. The event would start around one o'clock in the afternoon. Seemed like an odd time, we thought. But after a couple of them we understood why. You see, the Belgians value the time with their guests. It is an all-day affair to visit, serve food, have a few drinks and walk around their gardens. Time with relatives is precious and valued. Dish after dish is served. I didn't know you could prepare Belgian endives in so many ways. We would have shrimp, lamb, pork ribs, and chicken. It was incredible. And of course, then dessert would come out. But the eating was not rushed like back home. They didn't shove everything in and be done in ten minutes. All day went into preparations and all day was spent enjoying the fruits of the cook's labour.

First, wine or beer would be served upon arrival. Like I said, drinking beer and wine throughout the day in moderation is quite common, but not before lunch. Drinking too early is frowned upon by the Belgians. You must have a drinking problem if you start too early. After a drink was enjoyed, the first course would come out which could be soup or a small salad with bread. Then more time would pass with another glass of wine. About an hour or so later, the main courses would come out with meats, salads, and vegetables. Then more wine. More visiting and laughter. Still have room? Okay, now it's time to go back for seconds. And of course, there is still room for another kind of wine. But let us not forget dessert. Usually a type of fruit flan was served. Maybe room for more wine to finish off the evening. The event would go on for at least six hours. Maybe throughout this time, you may wander through the garden and pick fresh grapes off the vines. If they had chickens, you could throw them a grape or two. Why not share? Now, doesn't that sound like a better lifestyle than the way we gobble our food, slam a couple of drinks and go? Of course, every meal was not like this but every time we visited a relative, this was the royal treatment we were given. Can you see now why I'm glad all my pants were stretchy?

Eating this way taught us something. Food and family are meant to be enjoyed together. We always ate together as a family at home but it was always rushed, that is, until we got back from Europe. Hurry up and put the food on the table as soon as it's cooked. Hurry up and eat it before it gets cold. Hurry up and do the dishes. Our old way of eating was a stressful event and it shouldn't be. I would sometimes spend hours creating a meal only for it to be done and over in ten minutes. *Time for dishes.*

European eating culture has woven its way into our daily lives. We slowed down our eating style to fit in with the Belgians and we have brought this eating style back home with us. We didn't notice it until we sat down for a potluck lunch at our former church in Sylvan Lake. Darryl and I had arrived back to Canada and headed up to Sylvan to visit Brandon. We stayed with close friends from church so we went to church on Sunday morning.

Potluck lunch was served after church. Before our travels, I would be one of the first in line, eyeballing Darryl to get in line too before all the egg salad sandwiches are gone and he'd be left with Tuna, which he couldn't eat. This time, both Darryl and I were the last ones in line. We chatted and visited with friends while we waited for others to get their food. We got our food, sat down, and ate much slower than everyone else. A turtle's pace compared to the hare. I had only half my plate finished and everyone at my table had already finished dessert. Some people were even up and washing dishes already. *What's your hurry? It's Sunday and where do you have to be and why?* It was at that moment I promised myself to never eat fast again. It's not healthy and you miss the chance to visit with people who mean the world to you.

This didn't happen just at church. It would happen at restaurants too. Darryl and I would still be sitting and eating or finishing up a cup of coffee with brunch while the table next to us had been turned three times. *Why are we all so rushed?* Take the time and enjoy yourselves, people. There is a different way of life out there so get out there and learn about it. Don't let life pass you by because you insist on being so *busy*.

Chapter 21

Flanders Fields

Belgium stands out to me not only because of the hospitality shared with us from relatives but because of the tumultuous and fascinating history of the country. Belgium has been occupied by almost every country; perhaps that is why they are so tolerant of other cultures. Many ferocious battles of the world wars were fought in this tiny country.

The poem "In Flanders Fields" was written by a Canadian, and I heard this poem at every Remembrance Day ceremony in grade school. My parents always spoke of being proud Canadians and how they were honoured by the accomplishments of the Canadian soldiers in the World Wars. Flanders Fields was a must-see destination for both Darryl and I.

Ypres is a city in the Flanders region (the Belgians pronounce it Eeper). It was destroyed in World War I and many buildings have been carefully reconstructed to reflect the former splendour of the town. The beautiful buildings and unique Flemish architecture shine in the Belgian city of thirty-five thousand people. The Cloth Hall is a magnificent medieval reconstruction that dominates the huge town square. The building was destroyed in the war but now the cathedral-like appearance of the structure shines in all its grandeur, giving the square a palatial feel. No sign of the devastation brought on by the three Battles of Ypres remain to the naked eye.

The Flanders region stretches over 13,522 square kilometres. Flanders is an area straddling the Belgian provinces of East and West Flanders as well as the French department of Nord-Pas-de-Calais, or French Flanders. I imagined a single immense, green field covered in a contrast of poppies where battles had taken place. Equipped with our own car, we decided to drive the Salient route and see the memorial sites of World War I without a guide. I purchased a book at the Flanders museum that included a small map and explanations of the most important sites along the Salient route. After a delightful burger, fries and a Leffe beer at Ypres Burger Homestyle, Darryl and I mapped out which sites we wanted to see.

The Ypres Salient was a bulge in the front line of The Great War. The Germans occupied the ridges which formed a semi-circle around the city of Ypres. The British were at a disadvantage being overlooked on three sides from the high ground. Therefore, the area was a scene of repeated savage fighting since it was one of the most vulnerable sectors of the front. A breakthrough in the line would have meant catastrophic consequences for either side.

To drive the entire Salient route by car is 70 kilometres. We were sure we could see the major sites of interest in a few hours. Boy, were we wrong. It didn't take long to realize the impact of visiting the haunting sites and we knew we had to return to explore this evocative region.

Note to Self: Always plan to be at an attraction longer than expected. I get carried away with taking pictures.

First stop: the Menin Gate in the town of Ypres. The impressive monument is a few short blocks away from the town square. The massive British War Memorial was built to commemorate the fallen, unaccounted for in World War I. The names of over fifty-four thousand British Commonwealth soldiers are carved into the stone, echoing their sacrifice. The gate turned out to be too small for all those missing. The remaining names are listed on the memorial at the Tyne Cot Cemetery. To stand and reflect on all the names carved into the walls was humbling. These soldiers died for what we have today.

Numerous wreaths of poppies lie at the side gates of the memorial. Besides the laying of the wreaths, *The Last Post* has been sounded every night since 1928 at 8:00 p.m. The ceremony commemorates the sacrifice of the soldiers. First of all, wreaths are laid, hymns are sung, and the bugle trumpets out *The Last Post*. We planned to visit Ypres again to take in this moving experience.

Flanders Fields was made famous by the poem "In Flanders Fields." Lieutenant Colonel John McCrae of the Canadian Army Medical Corps wrote the poem near Essex Farm Cemetery. The poem was inspired by his experiences in the trenches. The bunkers where McCrae wrote the epic poem are accessible and remain near the cemetery where one thousand casualties of war are buried. The youngest soldier, 5750 Rifleman V.J. Strudwick, killed in the line of duty at the age of fifteen, is also laid to rest in the cemetery. A melancholy display of poppies and a teddy bear border his headstone.

The Brooding Soldier is the most poignant memorial we saw on the Salient route. The imposing granite column stands facing where a cloud from the first German gas attack took place. The stone soldier stands alone with his head lowered, leaning on a gun barrel. The extreme feeling of sadness seeps from the expressive stone-carved face. Eerily, the soldier seems to be keeping watch over the area where two thousand Canadian soldiers died in the attack. I stood at the foot of the statue and turned to face the direction he was facing, trying to picture what it would have been like for the men as they saw and smelled a weapon they had never encountered before. A pungent, irritating odour of bleach would have enveloped the area as the chlorine gas crept across the mud-pooled countryside. There was no way they could have saved themselves. I mourned alongside the soldier.

Time flew by. Sadly, we had to go before we could visit the Tyne Cot Cemetery. Darryl and I were deeply moved by what we had seen on this trip. We had visited two sites and it had taken most of the afternoon. We both agreed we had to return and see more. We felt a sense of patriotism that we had never experienced before. Seeing the beautiful green fields of today versus the destruction, death and debris of photos from the wars was striking.

A few weeks later, we picked up where we left off and continued our journey through a part of unforgettable Canadian and world history. The Tyne Cot Cemetery is the largest Commonwealth War Graves cemetery in the world, the final resting place of the eleven thousand nine hundred servicemen buried there. Some men still lie exactly where they were shot and killed. Gorgeous blood-red roses line the white granite headstones, a stark contrast and lasting remembrance of the blood shed on these lands. The cemetery is located on the scene of the Third Battle of Ypres, also known as the Battle of Passchendaele. Three German concrete bunkers remain inside the cemetery as unnerving ghostly remnants of war.

Darryl and I decided to walk the 3-kilometre trek to the village of Passchendaele from the cemetery. The path is the same path the Canadian soldiers marched to take the village from the Germans. Alone on the path, except for the odd cyclist, we headed out on our journey back in time. It was a calm, warm day. Cattle grazed in the pastures. The fields are now green and lush, nothing like the shattered countryside the soldiers faced. The corn fields are expansive. Dense stalks of corn stood at attention alongside the path. A Canadalaan (Canada Lane) sign along the path made us exceptionally proud of our past—a memorial from the Belgian people to our Canadian servicemen.

We arrived at the tiny village of Passchendaele about twenty minutes after our start. Directly to the left is the Passchendaele Canadian Memorial. The solid block of Canadian granite bares the inscription "The Canadian Corps in Oct-Nov 1917 advanced across this valley—then a treacherous morass—captured and held the Passchendaele Ridge." The village was completely wiped out in WWI. Now rebuilt, the quiet little town lies where Canadians had stormed cellars one by one, unearthing hidden German soldiers, sealing the Allied victory. The Canada Gate stands off to the side of the monument. A straight road representing the last 800 metres of Passchendaele secured by the Canadians directs your attention to a church. *If only more Canadians, especially the youth of today could experience these tremendous historical sites, they would appreciate what we have and what sacrifice was given for us.* The past came alive for us in Flanders Fields.

Eager to see more, we walked back to the Tyne Cot Cemetery, got back into our car and drove to Hill 60. Hill 60 was captured by the Germans from the French in 1914. Later, the British overtook this land and began the underground war of mines and counter-mines. Soldiers and miners worked for countless hours digging tunnels and setting explosives. Many died and were buried in the tunnels making Hill 60 a graveyard. Now a tranquil, pockmarked piece of land, Hill 60 is a reminder of the terrifying events from over a hundred years ago. Small sentries of concrete bunkers peek out of the ground. A short walk takes you to the infamous Caterpillar Crater, a result of a massive explosion from mines detonated in the Battle of Messines. The crater is now filled with water and is surrounded by green grass and trees.

In order to catch The Last Post ceremony at the Menin Gate back in Ypres, we had to leave and forego the other sites we wanted to see. We felt we had only scratched the surface of this incredible piece of land called Flanders. It would have been a shame to rush. This was a time for reflection and gratitude for all that had been sacrificed in the name of freedom.

People packed the Menin Gate to see The Last Post ceremony. As a result of arriving early, we had room to stand. At 8:00 p.m., the church bells rang, as they always do in Europe; a glorious sound to warm the heart. The ceremony commenced with a choir singing, "Be Still My Soul." Consequently, the crowd was silent. The Bugler of the Local Fire Brigade played "The Last Post." The sorrowful notes resonated through the tunnel and flowed over the names of the missing war dead, spilling out and rushing through the town of Ypres. Wreaths of remembrance were laid as the choir sang "Abide with Me". The daily act of remembrance brought people to tears. Darryl and I were silent. Goosebumps covered my body and I could feel a tightness of emotion in my chest.

The eleventh day, of the eleventh month of the eleventh hour, will never be the same for me. November 11, 1918, at 11:00 a.m. is the day the War to End all Wars was over. On Remembrance Day, we commemorate all war veterans for their sacrifice to their country. The wars throughout history have affected countless lives. Families traumatized. Bright, young lives taken too early. Horrors of the destruction of war burned into the memories of survivors. Measures had to be taken to stop tyranny and protect the rights and freedoms we cherish today.

War memorabilia dwells in my childhood home. My grandfather's hat from his service uniform sits on an antique pump organ in the living room at the farm. This hat is pristine. Why? Out of respect for my grandfather—because as he boarded the train headed east to Europe, World War I ended. *How would our lives have been different if Grandpa went to serve? Would he have come back? Possibly not. My father would not have been born and I would not be here today.*

I pray for peace in this broken world. We must not forget the brave women and men who gave their lives so we can have the freedom we enjoy today. Canada, and the world, please don't forget the soldiers' sacrifice.

Chapter 22

Belgium

Mornings with Ludo and Christiane brought a welcome consistency after being on the road for three months. Ludo was an early riser and awake at 5:30 a.m. As he put it, "First, I turn on the lights. Then I turn on the coffee. Then I turn on my computer. Then, music, because I cannot live without music."

Ludo and Christiane would wait for both of us before enjoying their morning meal. We were usually up by 7:30 a.m. That seemed to be our natural wake-up time. I did not miss waking up to an alarm. Daily breakfast consisted of toast, jam, assorted dried and cured meats and a selection of cheeses. And of course, coffee. One morning, Ludo surprised us with an American style breakfast of bacon, scrambled eggs and toast. He had never cooked such a meal before and he was quite proud of himself for his attempt. *His attempt was a complete success.*

Darryl and I would take our second cup of coffee outside to enjoy in the backyard. Belgian backyards are lovely with flowers and bee houses. Christiane had recently bought a small, decorative fountain of a boy pouring water into a bucket. The sound of the water only added to the peacefulness of the comfortable garden. The Belgians thought we were a little crazy for sitting outside in the cold. It was usually 15 degrees Celsius in the mornings—that's shorts and t-shirt weather for Canadians.

"How can we possibly go back to our old way of living?" I dreamily gazed at Darryl. We had come to treasure these moments in the garden with our coffee and books to read. "I want every morning to be like this. You and me, coffee, reading and no traffic to fight every morning."

"We can't." Darryl is not a man of many words. My strong, silent teddy bear. The laid-back life of our Belgian relatives and the other countries we had experienced in our travels had taken ahold of our hearts. Live in the moment. That's what the Belgians taught us.

At breakfast, Christiane would usually tell us what was going to be served for lunch or supper. Like me, she had a keen sense of planning. Every day, she would recite to us what family we were going to meet, who she had arranged for us to visit the next day, or what town they were going to explore with us next. They were thrilled we were there and I am sure she called every relative still on this side of the grass to meet us. It was awesome. Ludo once said to her, "We will put a string in your back and pull it so you can repeat yourself easier." Ludo had a wonderfully dry sense of humour. His face was quite serious but his sense of humour was priceless.

Christiane started to explain one particular meal to us that raised the alarm. "We are going to have the dark sausages." My eyebrows shot up. *Is she talking about what I think she is talking about? A meal we had avoided like the plague. Blood sausages.* She proceeded to describe the process of making the dark sausages, "Then they take the blooood." I shot a look in Darryl's direction. He was trying to mask the fear in his face, but I could see and feel it. The feeling was mutual. Christiane proceeded to tell us of this Belgian delicacy. I am not a picky eater. I will eat almost anything, but my stomach lurched. *How can we get out of this one?*

Note to Self: Be prepared to be served anything when in foreign countries and learn how to politely decline if you just can't eat it.

"Blood sausage doesn't really appeal to us," I said warily.

"But they are delicious," piped up Ludo. He was serious this time.

"I don't know…" Darryl's mouth curled up in a squeamish look.

"We can get white sausages to go along in case you don't like them." Christiane's compromise was a welcomed gesture.

"Okay, I will try one but just in case I don't like it, order me a white sausage too." I would give it the old college try because an alternative had been provided as a safety-net.

"I'll have the white sausages." Darryl was not going to venture too far from his comfort zone.

Ludo walked to the grocery store every day so Darryl and I went along this time. He wanted to show us where they get the dark sausages. Into the deli we went and it looked like a typical deli counter you would see in Canada. Darryl and I stood at the back of the room while Ludo looked left and right through the meat display window. He threw his hands up to shoulder height, palms facing the ceiling, "Whaaaat? No dark sausages?" Those were the sweetest words I'd heard in a long time. I looked at Darryl and he had a smile as big and wide as my own. We were saved. I think we even gave each other a high-five in that moment.

Note to Self: Even small victories are worth celebrating.

Tuesday evenings were special in Belgium. Diane, a friend of Ludo and Christiane's would come over for Cava, a drink similar to champagne but it cannot be called that because it is not from the Champagne region. Diane and I instantly clicked. Her short, brilliant white hair framed her lovely, tanned face. Diane is in excellent physical shape for her age. She is active, slim, trim and vibrant. Her English vocabulary was limited but Ludo and Christiane helped translate. It was such a joy to spend those evenings visiting. We had many laughs and bonds of friendship were made.

In Belgium, they take the time to establish lifelong friendships and keep in regular contact. They will camp together, ride bikes together, and walk together. In Canada, we always say, "Let's get together," but we never do. Everyone is always too busy to get together and commit to staying in touch.

Belgians think nothing of riding their bikes 60 kilometres or more in a day. Perish the thought in Canada. We just drive our cars. Ludo would go out for three-hour long walks just to walk "before it rains." Their culture is so incredibly laid back but, yet, so active.

Darryl's grandma took him to Belgium over thirty years ago to meet his relatives and see where he came from. His cousin, Johan, was thirteen at the time and Darryl was eighteen. Now, going back to see his relatives so many years later was a different experience for him. Johan is the same height as Darryl and the same build. Johan and his family were our own personal tour guides on a few occasions, even taking us to a soccer match in Antwerp. I guess I should say "football" lest they correct me. Darryl connected more with these people now than when he was eighteen due to his maturity. He knows he cannot wait another thirty years to go back again.

We spent four weeks with Ludo and Christiane and developed a close bond. They enjoyed our company as much as we enjoyed theirs, and we were sad to leave. I did not expect to establish such a bond. I had never met these people before and here they opened their homes to us and treated us like royalty. I am not a blood relative, but they treated me as if I were. To have lasting bonds with family on the other side of the world is, as the Belgians say, "something special." We were immersed in the Belgian culture and we wanted to bring it back to Canada with us.

We had been gone from Canada for what seemed like an eternity. Now the time was nearing to leave these wonderful people and this beautiful country so rich in history. As Darryl and I sat in the garden, we wondered how we could possibly go back to living the way we had before. We enjoyed the European way of life. What a gift to be so close to a plethora of countries and cultures. In an hour, you can cross three country borders. Not so in Canada. It can take seven hours to cross one province. There was so much we had seen but still so much that we wanted to take in with our own eyes. It was a bittersweet feeling as we missed Brandon and wanted desperately to see him, but now we were leaving another family behind. *When would we see them again?* The world had become our home; our identity now spanned borders, not just one country.

Part 3 – Metamorphosis

Chapter 23

A Monarch Emerged

Darryl and I were not excited to return to Canada. We loved our travelling lifestyle and were not looking forward to going back to the hurried mentality we left behind. The only thing drawing us back to the country was Brandon. We adore our son and it is hard being across the ocean from our only child.

Our first day back in Canada was the first day we had got on one another's nerves in a long time. We were both cranky and snappy with our remarks. It was clear that we were not ready to come down to reality. Canada had not changed, but we had. *Is this really where we want to stay? Now that we had such a rich taste of other countries and cultures, could we settle back down?* Canada is where our roots are. It is our home. It is where we should want to be.

Note to Self: Your home country will never be seen in the same light after an extended period of travel abroad.

We didn't want to rush at meals. The server would bring our bill before we were done eating. *Hurry up and get out,* was the message conveyed. Traffic was still crazy but we no longer got annoyed by it. We had become more patient and open-minded. Road rage was a thing of the past for us. *What's the hurry? We'll get there when we get there.* Our concept of time took a 360-degree turn. We still set the alarm during the week to get up and work from home to encourage some discipline in our lives, but it was much easier starting our day at 7:00 a.m. than at 5:00 a.m., only to be stuck in traffic.

Since returning from our extended travels to Europe, I have come to realize a few things. Getting ahead in this world and acquiring more and more material possessions only induces stress. We are groomed to think the more we buy, the happier we will be. I wholly disagree. Toys mean nothing. All the "stuff" collected over the years will end up in a garbage dump somewhere eventually, and it will all whither and rot away. I have come to realize the value of experiences and how they profoundly enrich life. Rather than the compounding stress of acquiring material things, good experiences melt the stress away. Contentment provides true security. I no longer feel the need to prove myself to others by acquiring more possessions. Insecurity had caused me to constantly seek approval from family and friends for all I said and did. That insecurity was left behind during my travels—buried on the other side of the ocean.

While travelling, we were figuring things out at our own pace. We were seeing new sites and learning new skills, like driving in foreign countries. Sure, we had some stressful moments, but we were learning to deal with those moments in new ways. I learned to chill out while Darryl was driving. I didn't get annoyed at him as quickly as I had at the beginning of the trip. My innermost being was calm. We were now living day-by-day, moment-by-moment. Most of the time we had no idea what day of the week it was, nor did we care. We still have to ask each other, "Is it Tuesday or Wednesday? What day of the week is it anyway?" Not worrying about anybody else's demands on our precious time was freeing. We had no TV to watch, no radio stations to listen to. It was the two of us all the time and it was good. We appreciated one another's company. It was us and the world.

People think we are off our rockers, and that is okay. I brush it off. "How long are you going to do this blog thing before you give up?" "What are you, nineteen years old again?" They get the answer, "I'm not giving up," or "Maybe." I have a perseverance I did not have before. A sense of purpose and joy in what I do every day. My creativity has flourished from all the sights, sounds and tastes I have had the privilege of experiencing. I find it easier to chat and interact with strangers. I no longer wake up in a cold sweat or look at the alarm clock every two hours, wishing I could have a good night's sleep. I now wake up and say, "Good morning, Lord" instead of "Good Lord, it's morning." I have a sense of contentment with who I am as a person. Has my desire to travel been quenched? Not in the least. I have a greater calling now to travel than I did before.

How I spend every morning has become a true treasure. My day starts with some push-ups and sit-ups before heading to the kitchen to brew Darryl and myself a cup of coffee. Most mornings I leave the bedroom to smell the rich earthiness of freshly ground beans that Darryl has ready for me. I must admit, Darryl makes better coffee than I do. After breakfast, we both sit and read a chapter from the *Bible*. We never seemed to have time for this before and now it has become habit. For at least an hour, we read other books to soak up knowledge and provide some entertainment. After all, we have reserved these early hours for our education time and these reading sessions set the tone for the rest of the day. I have always loved to read and now my mornings have become my favourite part of our new life.

Another transformation came when we realized that Saturday no longer had to be the weekend for us. We could pick and choose what days to work. If we want to go somewhere on Wednesday, we will make plans to work on Saturday instead. Sometimes it's better to get out midweek because the traffic is lighter and there aren't so many people out and about. It is easy enough to write and work on my blog any day that is convenient. I get lost in time when I write and dive into my photography. My efforts now energize my creativity. I cherish the freedom I have today. Each day, I have the privilege of sharing my travel stories, inspiring others to get out into the world and unfurl their wings.

As I write this portion of my book, I have had the pleasure of being in Texas for four months. Texas is a second home in my heart. I have great affection for the people, the food, and believe it or not, the weather. Yes, even when it's 40 degrees Celsius outside and you realize what a baked potato feels like. I have not found many places in my travels where strangers will strike up a conversation with you while waiting for the walk signal to change. But in Texas, it is the norm for people to start a conversation with, "How y'all doin' today?" And end the conversation with, "Enjoy your day." Being in Texas for an extended period of time has given me the opportunity to explore Hill Country to the fullest and live the positive energy of the towns nestled in the rolling hills carpeted with cedar and oak trees.

We have the freedom to volunteer for projects outside of Canada because we are not constrained to a weekly paid vacation regime. Our current lifestyle allows us to work and play from anywhere in the world. Having the globe as my office gives me the ability to explore and share my experiences in the world. Although I work harder and longer hours than I did before, I do it with zeal as I am pursuing *my* dreams and not someone else's.

We don't consider ourselves minimalists, but we now realize what is essential to live and enjoy in this life and what constitutes building up cheap treasures on this earth. There are more ways to live than to fall into the conformity of having a huge mortgage. We were quite happy in our apartments (well, the spacious ones, at least). The root of the word "mort-gage" is "death pledge." We were dying in our previous lives, constrained by everything tying us down. Without a mortgage, we are free to go and do whatever we want, whenever we want. We will settle down and grow up someday. I'm not sure if or when we will ever buy a house in Canada again, though. Prices are too over inflated. Neither Darryl nor I have a desire to have a $500,000+ mortgage. At our age, that truly is a death pledge.

Brandon says we are *different* than we were before we left. We wanted to make changes in our lives and in our attitudes; we had to do something radical. Change is the only thing that would make us grow. By experiencing other countries for an extended time period, we had to change, learn, and adapt. We were forced into situations we would otherwise never have experienced. If I had looked for a job after graduation, nothing would have changed and we would be living the exact same life as before. We would have fallen back into another rut after about six months. Exhausted from getting up early every morning to beat traffic. Not taking time for meditation and prayer because we had to rush out the door. Seeing each other for only a few hours a day during the week and counting the days until the weekend. Buying clothes for work. Packing lunches. Eating so fast we could hardly taste the food or appreciate the loving hands that prepared it. Being stressed out all the time. Waiting to turn sixty-five so we could retire. Being addicted to a paycheque. Only dreaming about places we wanted to see while saying, "Someday."

Going to the same desk every day following the exact same routine had been both numbing and a cause of anxiety for Darryl and me. Numbing in the fact we didn't care anymore. Anxiety inducing because of the constant pressures and stimulus, faced by the constant interruptions of ringing telephones and the endless dings indicating, "You've got mail." Everybody wanted an answer from us and they wanted it now. Pretty soon, we were a hot, sweaty mess, dreaming of Friday, the weekend, and a bottle of wine to escape the daily grind.

We would spend the week before leaving on our anticipated two-week vacation in a dream-state. Fantasizing of the perfect location, cocktail, and sunset. No work. No distractions. No boss. Finally, vacation day would arrive. During the first week, we were in a state of bliss, still maybe a little on edge from the stresses of our jobs. Then, as quickly as the first week arrived, it was gone. *Only one week left.* Only one week until we go back to the bowels of hell. Anxiety would start to pick up again as our thoughts would race back to work. *What's going to be on my desk when I get back?* The last week of our precious vacation was plagued with thoughts of somewhere we didn't want to return, but we had to. Then, the dreaded first day back to work. We would walk into the office and it felt like we were never gone. The rest of the week would go by and we were in a fog. Still in vacation mode and functioning just enough to get done what we had to do to stay employed. Sounds like an addiction, doesn't it? I'm starting to sweat just writing about it.

I look at problems differently now. I am more relaxed, and not nearly as high-strung as I used to be. Before our travels I found it difficult to accept mistakes, such as missing a turn in traffic. What used to be a disaster has now turned into a realization that we can take the next turn and get back on course. Before, I would get all huffy, tense up and furrow my brow. Now, I shrug and say, "Ah, just take the next corner. We will get back on track." Waiting in line at a restaurant is no longer a frustration. *What does it matter? We have nowhere to be by a specific time. Why not enjoy people watching and each other's company while we wait for our table?* My prior personality would have had me looking at my watch every five minutes and impatiently saying, "Good grief. How much longer is this going to take?"

I have become hyper-sensitive to people that are stressed out. A visit to the grocery store shows me the extent of my new superpower. People are ramming their carts down the aisle, pushing their way through other people as if they don't exist. *Get out of the way or you may be hurt; this is my grocery store.* There is only a faint window of time for people to achieve their errands. I understand, though, I used to be one of them. Mother's threaten their children to behave or they will be forced to go sit in the car. People gripe and complain when the lines are too long. Too many people in an aisle? Go down another one that is not so busy. Line too long? Check out the magazines nearby, perhaps aliens have landed and you didn't know it yet. Exposing myself to long-term travel has given me balance in my life and I have conditioned my brain to react differently to stress. The daily tasks that people rush through are now times that I live in the moment and take in all the craziness around me, grateful that I no longer act the way I used to.

Travel has taught me to use the gifts God has blessed me with and live this one life to the best of my ability. When my days are over, I will be spent. Being an entrepreneur is not easy and Darryl and I don't have all the answers yet, but we are determined to make it work and to live the rest of our lives this way. We are taking a risky leap of faith, but it is necessary in order to grow. We make sure to take two days off a week to rest and rejuvenate. We also make a point to get out and see other people. Conversation with other humans is important for our sanity.

Extra time is needed to deeply experience a country and learn from it. That is how we reinvented ourselves through travel. Two weeks doesn't cut it. No one is immune to the fear of change.

Living a life guided by fear only leads to boredom. We had to face our fears head on and step out of the doom and gloom of our daily grind to change the way we viewed life. Travel was our antidote to fear. Through travel, I discovered we are all equal in humanity but we are not equal in our abilities. There is genius in everyone. I just needed the freedom to find it.

Darryl and I are not nomads. We both still want and need a home. An anchor is important. We are now open to different ideas of what or where home can be. We reinvented our attitudes through travel; now we are rebuilding our lives. Travel has taken away our spirit of fear and replaced it with a spirit of peace, courage, and perseverance. Our focus has become one of serving the world rather than on the world serving us.

"Someday" is now our reality. We can literally work from anywhere on the planet. We enjoy each other's company. We don't drive the car every day so that's a bonus for the environment. I can't tell you how much joy it brings me to sit with my cup of coffee each morning while watching the morning traffic on the Calgary news and saying a silent prayer of thanks we are not in traffic for hours on end each day.

"When are you coming home, Charlotte?" is what Mom would have said to me when I told her of this new life we are living. She would listen intently while we visited, excited to hear about the funny stories that happened to us along the way. Mom didn't travel much so she would live her travel dreams precariously through me. She would love the pictures I took, especially of Venice. *Mom always wanted to see Venice.*

Mom would be proud of who I have become. A confident woman exploring the world on her own terms. She would also think our lifestyle was a little mad, like most people do. But, being my mother, she would still be my biggest fan, reading everything

I published and being the first person to like my updates on social media. *I miss her.*

My hope is that people who are not content with their lives or are unhappy with their current situation will take action to make meaningful changes. Life is too short to be miserable. There is so much good in this world and so many adventures to be had. By opening up to the possibilities of an unconventional lifestyle and exposing ourselves to different cultures through travel, we realize this world is a wonderful place. Travel is a powerful tool that offers us a chance to transform our lives. Travel can be more than just a dream. Start writing your own travel stories and connecting with people around this glorious planet that we call home. Who will you become and what qualities will you unleash in yourself once you take that leap?

Maybe you love to cook and have always wanted to master Italian cooking? Go to Italy and study the craft of their beautifully delicious and simplistic food. Want to learn another language? Pick a country that's native tongue is not English, buy your ticket, go, and master their vocabulary. Is there a cause in another country that speaks to your heart? Contact the organization and see how you can physically help on location. You may be surprised what opportunities are out there. The time is now. No more fears. Just go.

Acknowledgements

My friend, Hong Wang, invited me to an event in Calgary. "You should come. My publisher will be there. You should write a book." I told her writing a book was in my future plans, to which she enthusiastically responded, "I knew it." Maybe writing one sooner than later was the next challenge God had in store for me. I went to the event and met my publisher, Heather Andrews. I made a commitment that day to start my book. Thank you for the kick in the butt, Hong. And thank you, Heather, for believing in my story. Your team at Follow it Thru Publishing is magnificent.

I simply must thank Cari Frame, my structural editor, who challenged me to dig deep into my writing abilities and pull out thoughts from the recesses of my mind. Your suggestions were golden.

My biggest supporters have been the closest members of my family. Darryl, Brandon, Daren and Rita. I could never have done this without your unending encouragement.

To my teachers at SAIT, my fellow classmates that shared the love of travel, thank you for adding fuel to my desire of having my own travel business. What a difference it makes when like minds get together.

Mark Frentz, huge thanks for planting a crazy idea in my head. You spurned me to do something I had always wanted to do but thought was impossible. Thank you to our mastermind group that has also supported us on this journey from the moment Mark suggested it.

The biggest travel transformations and impact on Darryl and me were from the people we met and spent time with along the way. Our family in Belgium, dear Guido in Italy, and the other quirky folks that weaved their way into this tale.

Thank You, God, for the beauty of Your creation and the freedom to explore it.

About the Author

Charlotte Tweed, founder and author of the engaging travel blog, *A Wandering Web*, has always had a desire to travel and a love for the journey. When the opportunity arose to study Travel and Tourism at Southern Alberta Institute of Technology, Charlotte flourished in her new pursuits and graduated at the top of her class with Honours. Charlotte now uses her passion for writing and photography to inspire others to travel, often encouraging them to venture into extended travel so they get the most out of their holiday time, experience exceptional opportunities for personal development, and have adventures that genuinely enrich their lives.

Government restructuring empowered Charlotte to look beyond cubicle-life in the healthcare administration field and propelled her toward her long-time calling to be a travel-based entrepreneur. With her heart and her sights set on starting a travel business of her own, she and her husband sold almost everything they owned, put the rest in storage, and started travelling. They ventured to Texas, Egypt, Jordan, and a number of countries in Europe in search of a niche for her travel blog and business, and discovered a new mindset along the way.

After a courageous six-month foray into long-term travel, Charlotte's first book, *Roam Free*, was born. Charlotte loved the writing process and found it to be an educational and rewarding experience. Through collaboration with her publisher and editors, Charlotte's unique voice has grown along with her creativity. Evident in her blog, Charlotte is a gifted photographer as well, capturing the essence of the places she travels to and the people she meets. She has a keen eye for chronicling destinations in a distinctive way while conveying the story and relevant history of the location in an interesting and captivating manner.

Charlotte is a devoted wife and mother, an exploration pundit, and she loves to cook almost anything. She and her husband, Darryl, currently live in Calgary, Alberta where mornings are spent reading and enjoying the mountain-view while sipping a perfectly brewed cup of coffee.

Charlotte's social media

Facebook: https://www.facebook.com/groups/roamfree/

IG: https://www.instagram.com/awanderingweb/

Pinterest: https://www.pinterest.ca/awanderingweb/

Twitter: https://twitter.com/awanderingweb

LinkedIn: https://www.linkedin.com/in/charlotte-tweed-awanderingweb/

My Blogging Website: https://awanderingweb.com/

My Photography Website: https://portfolio.awanderingweb.com/